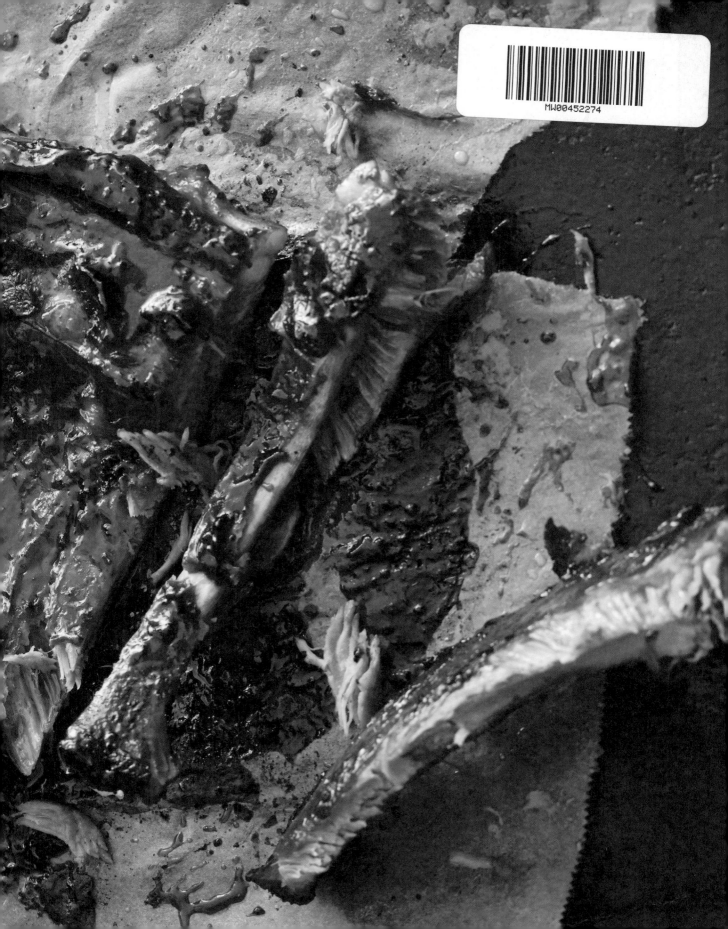

BOURBON, RIBS, AND RUBS

THE MAGIC OF COOKING LOW AND SLOW

CIDER MILL PRESS

BOOK PUBLISHERS

KENNEBUNKPORT, MAINE

13-Digit ISBN: 978-1-60433-962-8
10-Digit ISBN: 1-60433-962-4

This book may be ordered by mail from the publisher. Please include $5.99 for postage and handling.
Please support your local bookseller first!

Books published by Cider Mill Press Book Publishers are available at special discounts for bulk purchases in the United States by corporations, institutions, and other organizations.
For more information, please contact the publisher.

Cider Mill Press Book Publishers
"Where good books are ready for press"
PO Box 454
12 Spring Street
Kennebunkport, Maine 04046
Visit us online!
cidermillpress.com

Typography: Clarendon, Helvetica Neue, Giza
Image Credits: Page 7, courtesy of Library of Congress; page 12, courtesy of Buffalo Trace; pages 15 and 19, courtesy of Convenience West; page 16, courtesy of 12 Bones. Pages 4–5, 20–21, 46–47, 59, 102–103, 266–267 used under official license from Shutterstock.com. All other images courtesy of Cider Mill Press.
Front cover image: Rosemary Spareribs, see page 58
Back cover image: Sticky Baby Back Ribs, see page 36
Front endpaper image: Asian Spareribs, see page 67
Back endpaper image: Yuzu Sesame Lamb Ribs, see page 113

Printed in China
1 2 3 4 5 6 7 8 9 0
First Edition

CONTENTS

THE ORIGINS OF
BOURBON & BARBECUE

Named America's Native Spirit by Congress in 1964, bourbon is truly America's signature whiskey, and deeply intertwined with the history of its birthplace, Kentucky. Corn was a favorite crop of Kentucky's early pioneers, many of whom were immigrants of Scottish and Scots-Irish descent. Having brought the distillation techniques of their homeland with them, it was only a matter of time before they applied them to Kentucky corn.

Bourbon must be aged in new, charred oak barrels, lending the spirit a smokiness, as well as notes of caramel and vanilla; and a 51 to 80 percent corn mash bill is now enshrined as one of bourbon's defining features, which is what makes it notably sweeter than most whiskeys (one reason why it works so well in barbecue sauces). It also just so happens that when bourbon is used to flavor meat it not only imparts all those dynamic flavors found in a single expression, but it breaks down the enzymes and tenderizes the meat.

Unlike bourbon, barbecuing and smoking ribs is not an American invention—far from it. References to cooking meat low and slow over indirect heat can be traced to ancient China and the Bible. In the New World, the Taíno people of Hispaniola introduced Spanish explorers to the practice of using uncured wood to kindle slow-burning, indirect heat. The Spanish called this technique "barbacoa." A burgeoning American tradition was born, and quickly evolved into its own distinctive regional styles. Cinched into the American "barbecue belt," four traditions fit snuggly, and proudly: Carolina, Texas, Memphis, and Kansas City. No matter the region, all barbecue enthusiasts agree that it isn't barbecue if there isn't a grill involved.

Like sports teams, pizza, and sandwiches, people take their barbecue seriously. If you are in the Carolina camp, only pork qualifies as an appropriate protein (a tradition inspired by the food availble to the Spanish explorers as they colonized the New World. The colonists furthered this tradition as they settled). In Texas, beef is preferred for barbecue.

There is another, perhaps even more important factor in play: sauce. North Carolina is split between the vinegar-based recipes of the eastern part of the state and the ketchup-tinged sauces found in its western reaches. In South Carolina, mustard makes the scene; a "mop" is applied to Texas 'cue, doubling down on beef with beef broth; and the sweet, tomato-based Kansas City style is what was first bottled on a commercial scale.

All these variations are a direct result of how European colonization affected each region's cuisine, and today that change continues, which is why this book features a whole range of ribs recipes, both traditional and not. Sure, purists don't tend to stray from tradition, but there's a lot to be said for elevating tradition with innovation, as several of these recipes manage to do. Whether you want to boil the ribs first, grill them, smoke them, or roast them in the oven, you'll find something to satisfy your cravings in the recipes that follow, along with plenty of snacks and sides.

And there is a bounty of bourbon, too. For those who like their bourbon neat, or refuse to adorn it with anything more than an ice cube or two, they know what they're doing. But for those of you looking to spice up your repertoire there are delightful drink recipes peppered throughout the book to complement the ribs and the hours spent preparing them. After all, you should enjoy yourself as much as possible—that's what low and slow living is all about.

THE BOURBON EXPERTS

Here are three surefire traditional ways to give your ribs flavor, provided by whiskey expert Richard Thomas, author of American Whiskey and founder of The Whiskey Reviewer, as well as a go-to recipe that the good folks at Buffalo Trace use when they have a cookout.

BOURBON BARBECUE SAUCE

YIELD: 2 Cups **ACTIVE TIME:** 40 Minutes **TOTAL TIME:** 45 Minutes

With so many bourbon-flavored barbecue sauces on the market, one might wonder why making your own sauce from scratch is even necessary. The answer is simple: control. Making your own means enjoying full control over the end product. If you want something sweeter, take this recipe and add more sugar. Do you want something bolder? Try adding chipotle chili powder. If you like fruity flavors, add a little cherry or blueberry syrup. Another thing to consider is that some barbecue lovers live in a place where buying an imported, brand-name barbecue sauce is expensive, even if the individual ingredients are inexpensive and readily available.

For most people, the virtue of a recipe like this is its flexibility. Use it as a base to experiment with. Eventually, you will come up with your own secret sauce that will be a hit at every cookout you don the apron for.

My standing rule about cooking or making mixed drinks with bourbon is that using a fine bourbon is a waste, but using a bad bourbon ruins whatever you put on the menu. Steer clear of the rotgut and use middling bourbons in these recipes.

INGREDIENTS

2 tablespoons unsalted butter

2 large garlic cloves, diced

1 small yellow onion, diced

1 cup tomato sauce

1 tablespoon Worcestershire sauce

1 tablespoon white vinegar

1 tablespoon bourbon

1 tablespoon honey

⅓ cup packed brown sugar

2 teaspoons mustard powder

1 tablespoon chili powder

1 teaspoon kosher salt

1 teaspoon black pepper

1 Melt butter in a saucepan and sauté the garlic and onion until tender.

2 Add all other ingredients, starting with the liquids and then moving to the solids. Stir thoroughly, then simmer while covered for 20 to 30 minutes.

3 If using this sauce for basting and/or serving, it can be applied to ribs hot or at room temperature; it can also be made ahead and stored in the refrigerator for up to a week.

MAPLE & BOURBON BARBECUE SAUCE

YIELD: 3 Cups **ACTIVE TIME:** 3 Cups **TOTAL TIME:** 30 Minutes

Maple syrup and bourbon take a sauce already sweetened by brown sugar that extra mile for an irresistable smoky-sweetness. Flavors like this go best with pork.

INGREDIENTS

6 oz. tomato sauce
½ cup apple cider vinegar
½ cup maple syrup
¼ cup Worcestershire sauce
1 cup bourbon
½ cup packed brown sugar
1 tablespoon liquid smoke
2 teaspoons cayenne pepper
2 teaspoons sweet paprika
2 teaspoons garlic powder
2 teaspoons onion powder
1 teaspoon cumin
1 teaspoon mustard powder

1 Combine all of the ingredients in a pot over medium-low heat and whisk them together.

2 Simmer for 20 minutes, until the sugar has melted and combined with the other ingredients, while stirring periodically. Do not overheat the sauce, as it will cause most of the alcohol to evaporate.

BOURBON PORK MARINADE

YIELD: 1¼ Cups **ACTIVE TIME:** 10 Minutes **TOTAL TIME:** 10 Minutes

With its combination of sweetness and charred smokiness, bourbon was made for pork. That should come as no surprise to any student of Southern culture, since pork was, and is, the staple protein of the Old South. Think about southern hams, southern sausages, and the barbecue of North Carolina and Tennessee, or the myriad recipes for pork-flavored soups and stewed greens. Pork has always lent itself well to the sweet and smoky treatment, hence its high profile on the barbecue grill.

INGREDIENTS

¼ cup bourbon
⅓ cup soy sauce
2 tablespoons Worcestershire sauce
2 tablespoons water
1 tablespoon minced garlic
1 tablespoon dark honey or brown sugar
1 tablespoon vegetable oil

1 Combine all the ingredients in a bowl.

2 Marinate ribs, or any cut of pork for that matter, for at least 8 hours in the refrigerator.

BOURBON, RIBS, AND RUBS   11

BUFFALO TRACE RIBS

YIELD: 6 to 8 Servings **ACTIVE TIME:** 35 Minutes **TOTAL TIME:** 4 Hours and 45 Minutes

Buffalo Trace in Frankfort, Kentucky, knows a thing or two about bourbon; it produces Sazerac and Pappy Van Winkle, to name just two. But they also know ribs, as this recipe makes clear.

Turn your gas grill into a smoker by keeping the heat low and adding some soaked hickory wood chips. These smoky ribs are fall-off-the-bone tender and perfect paired with a stout.

INGREDIENTS

For the Ribs

1 tablespoon kosher salt

1 tablespoon black pepper

¼ cup packed brown sugar

2 tablespoons hot paprika

2 teaspoons garlic powder

1 (2½ to 3 lbs.) rack pork ribs, membrane removed and patted dry

1 cup hickory wood chips, soaked in water for 1 hour

Water in a disposable aluminum pan

For the Sauce

½ cup ketchup

¼ cup bourbon

2 tablespoons maple syrup

1 tablespoon molasses

1 teaspoon apple cider vinegar

1 teaspoon Worcestershire sauce

1 teaspoon smoked paprika

1 teaspoon garlic powder

1 teaspoon onion powder

1. In a small bowl, mix together the salt, pepper, brown sugar, hot paprika, and garlic powder. Apply the rub to the ribs, patting to make sure it adheres to the meat.

2. Set one burner of a gas grill to high. Drain the wood chips and place in the center of a large square of heavy-duty aluminum foil; fold over and secure the edges to make a packet. Poke several holes in the top to allow smoke to escape. Place the packet over the heating burner and close lid until smoke starts billowing out; reduce heat to medium-low (about 250°F to 300°F).

3. Place the pan of water over the burner. Place the rack of ribs, bone-side down, over the burner that is not turned on; close lid.

4. Cook for 3½ hours. Flip over and allow to cook another hour or until tender enough to fall off the bone.

5. Meanwhile, in a saucepan over medium heat, mix together the ketchup, bourbon, maple syrup, molasses, vinegar, Worcestershire, paprika, garlic powder, and onion powder until it reaches a low boil. Reduce heat to low and allow to simmer 15 to 20 minutes, until slightly reduced.

6. Baste the ribs with sauce during the last 15 minutes of cooking.

7. When the ribs are done, let rest under a tent of aluminum foil for 15 minutes before separating the ribs and serving.

THE RIBS EXPERTS

Great ribs can be found all over, and with this book you too can count yourself among the ranks of folks who turn out succulent, flavorful ribs. But consistently making exceptional ribs does require some technique and practice, a hallmark of a professional pit master. Here are some tips and recipes from two celebrated barbecue joints that know their way around a grill.

12 BONES

All barbeque traditions mingle at 12 Bones Smokehouse in Asheville, North Carolina. Since opening its first location on the French Broad River in 2005, plenty has changed in this mountain town, but not the core commitment to making everything from scratch. Today, there is a second 12 Bones right outside of town, which only means there's twice the amount of amazing barbeque available if you are in the area. And if you don't find yourself in western North Carolina, make your own ribs using the 12 Bones Blueberry-Chipotle Barbecue Sauce, which is as close as you can get to this distinctly Asheville 'cue.

12 BONES BLUEBERRY-CHIPOTLE BARBECUE SAUCE

YIELD: 5 Cups **ACTIVE TIME:** 30 Minutes **TOTAL TIME:** 1 Hour

This sauce starts out sweet, but the finish is all chipotle. And the rich, smoky flavor ripens the longer you leave the sauce in the bottle. If you don't open it for at least a year, the smoke intensifies even further.

INGREDIENTS

1 pound fresh or frozen blueberries

5 oz. chipotle peppers in adobo sauce

¾ cup honey

3 cups 12 Bones Tomato "Q" Sauce (see recipe)

1 teaspoon ground ginger powder

1 In a food processor or a blender, puree the berries and the chipotles.

2 Transfer the berries and peppers to a saucepan, and add the remaining ingredients. Simmer this mixture over low heat for 30 minutes, stirring occasionally.

3 Remove the sauce from the heat and cool. The finished and cooled sauce can be stored in an airtight container in the refrigerator for up to a month.

12 BONES TOMATO "Q" SAUCE

YIELD: 4 Cups **ACTIVE TIME:** 15 Minutes **TOTAL TIME:** 35 Minutes

Make this for the Blueberry-Chipotle Barbecue Sauce, but be sure to experiment with this foundational element of many 12 Bones signature flavors.

INGREDIENTS

3 cups ketchup

²⁄₃ cup cider vinegar

½ cup blackstrap molasses

6 tablespoons Worcestershire sauce

6 tablespoons dark brown sugar

1 teaspoon granulated garlic

1 teaspoon granulated onion

1 teaspoon dry English mustard

1 teaspoon black pepper

1 teaspoon kosher salt

1 Combine all ingredients in a medium-sized saucepan and simmer on low heat until all of the dry ingredients have dissolved, stirring occasionally with a whisk. Note that mustard powder can be a bit hard to dissolve.

CONVENIENCE WEST

Marfa, Texas, has long been known as a waystation for artists, but was never known for barbecue. That is, until Convenience West opened in 2017. Chef Mark Scott and his partners bring their fine-dining expertise to the sides—sweet potato salad, blue corn cornbread, mac and cheese spiked with green chiles, cotija cheese, and cilantro—but when it comes to the ribs coming off the smoker there's only one rule: Keep it real simple.

In Scott's words, here's how the magic happens: "Our pork rib rub is simple: 50/50 mix of salt and pepper, and brown sugar. That's it! We cook them for 4 hours, then spray them with apple cider vinegar and wrap in butcher paper for another 2 hours, give or take. We smoke with oak at about 250°F. Pro tip for pork ribs: put the salt and pepper down first, then the brown sugar. The sugar caramelizes the salt and pepper on to the ribs and makes a great crust. Beef ribs get 50/50 salt and pepper and go on for about 9 hours."

PORK RIBS

PORK IS THE cornerstone of barbecue, with a juicy tenderness that can easily marry itself to sweet and savory flavors. The best pork ribs embrace this versatility, taking on the sweetness of brown sugar or the kick of chipotle, all without overpowering the naturally outstanding flavors of the meat.

SMOKED PORK RIBS

YIELDS: 4 Servings **ACTIVE TIME:** 3 Hours **TOTAL TIME:** 24 Hours

Any barbecue sauce works well in this recipe, particularly brown sugar- or molasses-based sauces. See page 10 for two bourbon-infused options.

INGREDIENTS

⅓ cup brown sugar

1 tablespoon chili powder

1 tablespoon smoked paprika

1 tablespoon black pepper

1 tablespoon garlic powder

2 teaspoons kosher salt

1 teaspoon ground cumin

1 (5-lb.) rack pork spareribs, cleaned

2 cups wood chips, e.g. applewood or cherrywood

2 cups barbecue sauce of your choosing

2 scallions, sliced (optional)

1 large red chile pepper, seeded and minced (optional)

1. In a small bowl, stir together the brown sugar, chili powder, paprika, black pepper, garlic powder, salt, and cumin.

2. Place the ribs on a roasting trivet set inside a baking dish lined with aluminum foil. Rub the spice mix into the ribs, cover the dish with foil, and refrigerate overnight.

3. The next day, preheat a gas grill, charcoal grill, or a smoker to 250°F. Soak the wood chips in a bowl of water.

4. If using a gas grill, place half of the wood chips in a packet of aluminum foil and place over the burner. Close the lid until smoke comes billowing out. If using a charcoal grill or a smoker, place half of the wood chips directly onto the coals when they are grey. Place the ribs on the grill, bone-side down.

5. Cover and cook until very tender, about 3 hours, adding more coals to the charcoal grill or smoker as needed to maintain its temperature and generously basting with the barbecue sauce; add more wood chips periodically as needed to maintain the smoke.

6. When the ribs are ready, remove from grill or smoker and garnish with scallions and the chile pepper, if using.

BOURBON-SPIKED SPARERIBS

YIELDS: 4 Servings **ACTIVE TIME:** 30 Minutes **TOTAL TIME:** 1 Hour and 30 Minutes

This is a traditional preparation that hits all the right barbecue notes: sweet up front with a little bite as it goes down.

INGREDIENTS

4 lbs. pork spareribs, trimmed and separated

2 onions, 1 halved, 1 diced

2 garlic cloves, 1 halved, 1 crushed

2 tablespoons canola oil

1 teaspoon kosher salt, plus more to taste

½ cup beef stock (for homemade, see page 274)

Juice of ½ orange

¼ cup ketchup

2 tablespoons soy sauce

2 tablespoons bourbon

1 tablespoon hot mustard

1 tablespoon Worcestershire sauce

1 tablespoon paprika

½ lemon, juiced

1 tablespoon peeled and chopped fresh ginger

½ teaspoon black pepper

1 dash Tabasco™

1. Place the ribs in a stockpot and cover with boiling water. Add the halved onion and garlic clove and simmer for 30 minutes.

2. Heat the oil in a pan and sauté the diced onion and the crushed garlic with a pinch of salt for 3 minutes. Stir in the stock and orange juice.

3. Cook until slightly reduced, then transfer to a bowl and stir in the remainder of the ingredients.

4. Once 30 minutes have passed, remove the ribs from the simmering water and pat dry with paper towels.

5. Preheat a gas or charcoal grill to 350°F. Brush the ribs with the barbecue sauce and grill for 10 to 15 minutes until lightly caramelized, turning the ribs and basting with more sauce from time to time.

6. Remove from grill and let rest briefly before serving.

BOURBON SAUCE SPARERIBS

YIELDS: 4 Servings **ACTIVE TIME:** 30 Minutes **TOTAL TIME:** 10 Hours

This is another classic approach to ribs, enhanced by the addition of cinnamon.

INGREDIENTS

For the Barbecue Sauce
½ cup brown sugar

½ cup unsalted butter, at room temperature

⅓ cup bourbon

¼ cup apple cider vinegar

2 tablespoons Dijon mustard

¼ teaspoon kosher salt

¼ teaspoon black pepper

For the Ribs
1 tablespoon kosher salt

1 tablespoon brown sugar

1 teaspoon mustard powder

1 teaspoon dried thyme

1 teaspoon smoked paprika

1 teaspoon ground ginger

1 pinch cinnamon

1 (3-lb.) rack pork spareribs, trimmed

3 garlic cloves, crushed

1 tablespoon peeled and thinly sliced fresh ginger

2 fresh bay leaves, or 3 dried bay leaves

1½ cups apple cider

---

1. To prepare the sauce, place all of the ingredients in a small saucepan and warm over low heat, while whisking frequently, until smooth and reduced slightly. Remove from heat and set aside.

2. To begin preparations for the ribs, whisk together the salt, sugar, mustard powder, thyme, paprika, ginger, and cinnamon in a mixing bowl.

3. Remove membrane from underside of ribs; loosen at ends with a paring knife and pull away by pulling at the edges.

4. Rub about 1 tablespoon of seasoning mix into both sides of the ribs. Place in a large roasting pan, cover, and refrigerate for at least 6 hours, preferably longer.

5. After chilling, preheat oven or grill to 325°F. Remove the ribs from the pan and add garlic, ginger, bay leaves, and apple cider, stirring well. Return the ribs to the pan, meat-side down, and cover the pan with aluminum foil.

6. Roast until the meat is tender and coming away from bones, about 2 hours. Remove from the oven or grill and let cool, uncovered, for 1 hour.

7. Preheat a gas or charcoal grill to a moderately hot temperature, about 425°F. Grill the ribs until lightly charred, turning a few times, about 12 to 15 minutes in total; baste frequently with the prepared sauce.

8. Remove the ribs when ready and let rest under aluminum foil for at least 10 minutes. Brush with more sauce before cutting the ribs between the bones.

RISE & SHINE

You're up early so things will be ready when everyone shows up for lunch and the start of the game. You've already made coffee or tea and opened a bottle of bourbon. Why not mix the two?

FAMILY MEAL

¼ part cold brew coffee concentrate

1½ parts Maker's Mark bourbon

Mexican Coca-Cola, to top

1 strip of lemon peel, for expression

1 Place the coffee concentrate and the bourbon in a rocks or highball glass, add ice, and stir gently. Top with the cola and express the lemon peel over the cocktail.

CHAI TODDY

6 oz. chai concentrate

2 oz. bourbon

Splash of hot water

1 Place the chai concentrate in a tea kettle and warm according to the manufacturer's instructions. Place the bourbon in a mug, pour the hot chai on top, and finish with the splash of hot water.

DIRTY WATER

1½ oz. green mint tea

3 to 4 sprigs fresh mint

1 oz. bourbon

½ oz. simple syrup

1 lemon wedge, for garnish

1 Place all of the cocktail ingredients in a cocktail shaker filled with ice and shake vigorously. Do not strain, but pour the contents of the shaker into a Collins glass filled halfway with ice and garnish with the lemon wedge.

ALL-AMERICAN SPARERIBS

YIELDS: 4 to 6 Servings **ACTIVE TIME:** 1 Hour **TOTAL TIME:** 24 Hours

Orange juice holds this sauce together with the natural sugars and citric tang.

INGREDIENTS

2 (3-lb.) racks pork spareribs, separated into four pieces

2 garlic cloves, crushed

½ cup tomato paste

⅓ cup ketchup

⅓ cup honey

¼ cup orange juice

¼ cup apple cider vinegar

¼ cup soy sauce

¼ cup bourbon

2 tablespoons Worcestershire sauce

1 teaspoon peeled and grated fresh ginger

½ teaspoon black pepper

1 Place the ribs in a large roasting pan.

2 In a mixing bowl, combine the remaining ingredients, stirring until the honey dissolves. Pour half over the ribs, turning to coat. Cover and refrigerate overnight.

3 The next day, preheat a gas or charcoal grill to 300°F. Place the ribs on the grill, cover, and cook for 3 hours, turning several times until the ribs are very tender. Remove from grill and increase temperature to 450°F.

4 Return the ribs to the grill, cooking and basting with the remaining sauce until lightly caramelized, about 10 to 15 minutes; turn from time to time.

5 Remove the ribs from the grill to a platter and serve.

APPLE CIDER
SPARERIBS

YIELDS: 4 Servings **ACTIVE TIME:** 1 Hour **TOTAL TIME:** 7 Hours

The natural sugars in the apple cider are the star of this recipe.

INGREDIENTS

1 (3-lb.) rack pork spareribs, trimmed

3 cups apple cider, plus more as needed

2 lemons, juiced

½ cup dry rub of choice

1 cup Maple Bourbon Barbecue Sauce (see page 10)

Fresh cilantro, chopped, for garnish

1   Place the ribs in a shallow roasting pan and pour apple cider and lemon juice over them, turning several times to coat. Cover and refrigerate for 2 hours.

2   Drain the ribs and pat dry with paper towels. Sprinkle dry rub on both sides of the ribs, pressing it into the meat with your fingers. Cover and refrigerate for 2 hours.

3   Preheat a gas or charcoal grill to 300°F. Place the ribs on the middle of the grill, cover, and cook until the meat is tender, about 2½ hours; spray the ribs every 30 minutes with additional apple cider.

4   After 2 hours, lightly brush the ribs with barbecue sauce. When the ribs are fully cooked, the meat will be tender enough to pull away from the bone.

5   When ready, remove the ribs from the grill and let rest under aluminum foil for 10 minutes. Garnish with a sprinkle of chopped cilantro and serve.

STICKY BABY BACK RIBS

YIELDS: 4 Servings **ACTIVE TIME:** 30 Minutes **TOTAL TIME:** 24 Hours

Baby back ribs get their name because of how they are butchered. Also known as back ribs, they come from where the ribs connect with a pig's spine, and are shorter than spareribs, hence the diminutive colloquialism. No matter the size, it's a meaty and delicious cut, enhanced here by lime zest and fresh thyme.

INGREDIENTS

Juice of 4 limes

2 tablespoons lime zest

2 red chile peppers, sliced

⅓ cup sugar

¼ cup olive oil

8 sprigs fresh thyme, roughly torn

6 garlic cloves, crushed

1 tablespoon kosher salt

1 teaspoon black pepper

4 lbs. baby back pork ribs

1. In a mixing bowl, thoroughly stir together the lime juice, lime zest, chile peppers, sugar, olive oil, thyme, garlic, salt, and black pepper.

2. Place the ribs on a large cutting board, meat-side down. Remove the membrane by loosening the ends with a paring knife and pulling away at edges.

3. Divide the ribs between large resealable bags, pouring marinade on top, reserving some for later. Remove excess air before sealing and refrigerate overnight.

4. The next day, preheat the oven or grill to 300°F. Remove the ribs from the marinade and arrange on a roasting trivet set inside a large roasting pan lined with aluminum foil. Pour reserved unused marinade into a saucepan and cover until needed.

5. Bake the ribs until very tender, about 2½ hours. Transfer from the dish to a platter, covered loosely with aluminum foil.

6. Bring the reserved marinade to a boil over a high heat and reduce by about half.

7. Preheat the broiler to high or grill to 450°F. Broil or grill ribs until caramelized and lightly charred, turning once, about 6 to 8 minutes in total; baste with reduced marinade from time to time.

8. Transfer the ribs to a serving platter and cut into portions before serving.

TEXAS BABY BACK
RIBS

YIELDS: 4 Servings **ACTIVE TIME:** 2 Hours **TOTAL TIME:** 15 Hours

A simple sauce really puts the meat front and center.

INGREDIENTS

2 tablespoons paprika

½ teaspoon cayenne

2 tablespoons garlic powder

2 teaspoons kosher salt

1 teaspoon black pepper

5 lbs. baby back pork ribs, trimmed

1½ cups ketchup

½ cup hot water

2 tablespoons molasses

1 In a mixing bowl, combine the paprika, cayenne, garlic powder, salt, and pepper.

2 Place the ribs in a shallow roasting pan and thoroughly apply dry rub to the ribs. Cover and refrigerate for at least 8 hours.

3 After chilling, remove the ribs from the fridge. Preheat a gas or charcoal grill to 300°F.

4 Grill the ribs for about 2 hours, covered, until the meat is tender and pulls away from the bones.

5 As the ribs cook, in a mixing bowl, stir together the ketchup, water, and molasses. Periodically brush the ribs with the prepared sauce, reserving any sauce that goes unused.

6 Remove the ribs from grill when ready and let rest under aluminum foil for 10 minutes.

7 Cut the ribs into portions. Spoon the reserved sauce into individual ramekins and serve.

HONEY-ROASTED BOURBON RIBS

YIELDS: 4 Servings **ACTIVE TIME:** 2 Hours **TOTAL TIME:** 7 to 24 Hours

These ribs get wonderfully caramelized thanks to the sticky-sweetness of both honey and molasses.

INGREDIENTS

½ cup honey

½ cup ketchup

¼ cup apple cider vinegar or distilled white vinegar

2 tablespoons molasses

2 tablespoons bourbon

3 star anise pods, lightly crushed

4 teaspoons Dijon mustard or hot mustard

1 pinch red pepper flakes

3 tablespoons olive oil

2 teaspoons kosher salt

1 teaspoon black pepper

4 lbs. baby back pork ribs, cleaned and trimmed

1   In a mixing bowl, combine all ingredients, except the ribs, and stir until the honey dissolves.

2   Place the ribs on a roasting trivet set inside a large roasting pan lined with aluminum foil. Coat thoroughly with half the marinade and chill for at least 4 hours or overnight.

3   When ready to cook, preheat the oven or grill to 300°F.

4   Cook the ribs until the meat falls from the bone, about 3 hours; baste with reserved marinade from time to time.

5   When ready, remove the ribs and let cool. Preheat the broiler to high or grill to 450°F.

6   Separate the ribs and caramelize under the broiler or on the grill for about 3 to 5 minutes, turning once.

DEVIL SAUCE SPARERIBS

YIELDS: 4 Servings **ACTIVE TIME:** 15 Minutes **TOTAL TIME:** 1 Hour and 30 Minutes

The bite of chile peppers, bourbon, vinegar, and Tabasco™ is undeniable here, but the honey tempers it, resulting in a tangy glaze that still keeps the pork in the spotlight.

INGREDIENTS

2 red chile peppers, seeded and chopped

1 onion, chopped

3 garlic cloves, chopped

⅓ cup honey

2 tablespoons bourbon

1 teaspoon kosher salt

½ teaspoon black pepper

¼ cup tomato paste

¼ cup red wine vinegar

1 dash Tabasco™

¾ cup water

4 lbs. pork spareribs, trimmed and separated

Sunflower oil, for brushing

1 In a saucepan, combine the chile peppers, onion, garlic, honey, bourbon, salt, black pepper, tomato paste, vinegar, Tabasco™, and water, and stir. Bring to a boil over high heat and then reduce to a simmer until smooth and thick, about 10 minutes. Remove from heat and set aside to cool.

2 Preheat a gas or charcoal grill to 350°F. Brush the ribs with a little oil and place them on the grill, cooking for about 40 minutes, turning occasionally. Baste the ribs with the prepared sauce about 10 minutes before they are ready.

3 Remove from grill and let cool briefly before serving.

ADOBO-BOURBON SPARERIBS

YIELDS: 4 Servings **ACTIVE TIME:** 1 Hour **TOTAL TIME:** 4 Hours

Using adobo sauce in any dish is an easy and effective way to add smoky heat to food, which makes it ideal for ribs.

INGREDIENTS

2 tablespoons olive oil

1 large yellow onion, chopped

3 garlic cloves, minced

3 tablespoons chopped chipotle chile peppers

½ cup red wine vinegar

2 tablespoons fresh lime juice

3 tablespoons adobo sauce

4 cups tomato sauce

⅓ cup molasses

3 tablespoons bourbon

2 teaspoons mustard powder

2 dried bay leaves

1 tablespoon kosher salt, plus 1 teaspoon

2 (3-lb.) pork sparerib racks, trimmed

2 tablespoons liquid smoke

2 tablespoons brown sugar

2 tablespoons paprika

1 tablespoon chili powder

1 tablespoon black pepper

1 teaspoon cayenne pepper

2 limes, halved

---

1 Heat the oil in a saucepan set over medium heat. Add the onion and cook until lightly browned, about 5 minutes.

2 Stir in the garlic and chiles, cooking for 1 minute. Deglaze the pan with vinegar and lime juice, and cook until the liquid has reduced by half, 1 to 2 minutes.

3 Stir in the adobo sauce, tomato sauce, molasses, bourbon, mustard powder, bay leaves, and 1 teaspoon salt. Bring to a simmer and cook until thick, stirring occasionally, about 15 to 20 minutes. Remove from heat and strain into a bowl.

4 Place the ribs in a stockpot. Cover with water and add the liquid smoke. Bring to a boil over high heat and then reduce to a simmer for 15 minutes. Remove from heat and drain on paper towels.

5 In a bowl, combine the sugar, paprika, chili powder, black pepper, cayenne, and 1 tablespoon salt. Pat the ribs with more paper towels before rubbing the spice mixture into them.

6 Preheat a gas or charcoal grill to 350°F. Place the ribs on the grill, cover, and cook for 10 minutes, turning halfway through. Reduce heat to 300°F.

7 Brush the ribs with the prepared sauce, cover, and cook for a further 2 hours, or until the ribs are very tender.

8 When ready, remove the ribs and rest under aluminum foil for 10 minutes. Cut between the bones to separate and serve with the lime halves on the side.

MOLASSES & MAPLE SYRUP COUNTRY-STYLE PORK RIBS

YIELDS: 4 Servings **ACTIVE TIME:** 25 Minutes **TOTAL TIME:** 2 Hours

Country-style ribs are a thicker alternative to spareribs, ideal for baking. They can be purchased as separate ribs or in a rack. If you buy a rack, separate the ribs before Step 1.

INGREDIENTS

3 lbs. bone-in, country-style pork ribs

¾ cup real maple syrup

½ cup ketchup

2 tablespoons fresh lemon juice

1 teaspoon Worcestershire sauce

½ teaspoon kosher salt

½ teaspoon paprika

¼ teaspoon ground cinnamon

¼ teaspoon black pepper

1 pinch cayenne pepper

1   Place the ribs in a large stockpot and cover with water. Bring to a boil over a high heat and then reduce heat and simmer for 10 minutes.

2   Remove from the pot and set on paper towels. Pat the ribs dry and then place them in a large oval baking dish and set aside until needed.

3   Preheat the oven or grill to 325°F. Whisk together the remaining ingredients in a mixing bowl before pouring over the ribs, turning to coat.

4   Roast until the ribs are tender with the meat coming away from the bones, about 1½ hours, basting from time to time with the sauce.

5   Remove from the oven or grill and let stand for 5 minutes before serving.

LEMONGRASS SPARERIBS

YIELDS: 4 Servings   **ACTIVE TIME:** 1 Hour   **TOTAL TIME:** 24 Hours

That lemony, minty flavor you can't quite put your finger on? It's lemongrass, and it adds a great dynamic to this recipe.

INGREDIENTS

2 garlic cloves, minced

1 small onion, minced

½ cup tomato paste

¼ cup ketchup

⅓ cup honey

⅓ cup orange juice

¼ cup apple cider vinegar

¼ cup soy sauce

2 tablespoons Worcestershire sauce

1 teaspoon peeled and finely grated fresh ginger

1 stalk fresh lemongrass, minced

4 lbs. pork spareribs, trimmed

½ cup fresh cilantro, finely chopped

1. In a mixing bowl, combine everything apart from the ribs and cilantro, stirring thoroughly. Divide the marinade in half, reserving one half for basting.

2. Generously brush both sides of the ribs with the remaining marinade, reserving any unused marinade for basting. Cover and refrigerate the ribs for at least 12 hours, turning the ribs over from time to time.

3. The next day, preheat a gas or charcoal grill to 300°F.

4. Place the ribs on the center of the grill, cover, and cook until the meat is tender, about 2 hours. About 20 to 30 minutes before serving, baste with the remaining marinade.

5. Transfer the ribs to a cutting board and let rest under aluminum foil for 10 minutes before cutting into individual or 2-rib sections.

6. Sprinkle the cilantro on top and serve.

TERIYAKI PORK RIBS

YIELDS: 4 Servings **ACTIVE TIME:** 30 Minutes **TOTAL TIME:** 2 Hours and 30 Minutes

American-style barbecue sauces rely heavily on ketchup. Using sauces that aren't built around tomato takes ribs to a whole other level.

INGREDIENTS

For the Ribs

1 (4-lb.) rack pork spareribs, trimmed

1 tablespoon brown sugar

1 teaspoon kosher salt

¼ teaspoon black pepper

2 teaspoons sesame oil

For the Glaze

1 tablespoon canola oil

4 star anise pods

1 tablespoon peeled and minced fresh ginger

1 garlic clove, minced

3 red chile peppers, sliced thin

¼ cup honey

3 tablespoons soy sauce

1½ tablespoons rice vinegar

1 teaspoon sesame oil

1 teaspoon cornstarch, mixed to a slurry with 2 tablespoons water

1 small handful fresh cilantro, torn, for garnish

1. To begin preparations for the ribs, bring an oven or grill to 325°F. Place the ribs on a roasting trivet set inside a large roasting pan lined with aluminum foil.

2. Stir together the sugar, salt, black pepper, and sesame oil in a small bowl. Rub the mixture all over the ribs.

3. Roast the ribs in the oven or on the grill until the ribs are browned and tender, about 2 hours.

4. To prepare the glaze, heat the canola oil in a saucepan set over medium heat. Stir in the star anise, frying for 30 seconds until fragrant. Add in the ginger, garlic, and chiles, cooking and stirring until fragrant, about 2 minutes. Stir in the honey, soy sauce, vinegar, and sesame oil.

5. Bring to a boil and then whisk in the cornstarch slurry, cooking until slightly thickened and reduced, about 2 to 4 minutes. Set aside.

6. Remove the ribs from oven or grill when ready. Preheat the broiler to high or the grill to 425°F.

7. Brush the ribs with half of the glaze, cooking under the broiler or on the grill until sticky and lightly caramelized, about 10 to 15 minutes; baste with the remaining glaze from time to time.

8. Remove the ribs and let stand briefly before serving garnished with the cilantro.

CHINESE-STYLE PORK RIBS

YIELDS: 4 Servings **ACTIVE TIME:** 10 Minutes **TOTAL TIME:** 1 Hour

---

Not as sweet as balsamic vinegar, Chinese black vinegar is made from glutinous rice and malt, which imparts a complex, fruity quality to the flavor, and to these ribs.

INGREDIENTS

3 lbs. pork ribs, trimmed and separated

¼ cup canola oil

1 shallot, finely chopped

2 garlic cloves, minced

3 tablespoons peeled and minced fresh ginger

¼ cup packed brown sugar

¼ cup maple syrup

⅓ cup Shaoxing wine

⅓ cup Chinese black vinegar

½ cup light soy sauce

1 Place the ribs in a large pot and cover with water. Bring to a boil and then simmer for 20 minutes.

2 Pour the oil into saucepan over medium heat and add the shallot, frying for 5 to 8 minutes. Stir in the garlic and ginger and fry for a few minutes.

3 Stir in the sugar, maple syrup, Shaoxing wine, vinegar, and soy sauce. Bring to a simmer and cook until reduced and thickened.

4 Once 20 minutes have passed, drain the ribs and let cool, patting dry with paper towels.

5 Preheat a gas or charcoal grill to 325°F. Place the ribs on the grill and cook until the meat is very tender and lightly charred all over, about 15 to 20 minutes, basting with the reduced sauce every 2 to 3 minutes.

6 When ready to serve, transfer the ribs to a platter and brush with the remaining sauce before serving.

KOREAN-STYLE PORK RIBS

YIELDS: 4 Servings **ACTIVE TIME:** 30 Minutes **TOTAL TIME:** 7 Hours

There is impressive depth to the soy-sweet flavoring in play here, and there is nothing spicy about it for those not inclined to such things.

INGREDIENTS

4 lbs. pork spareribs, trimmed

2 garlic cloves, minced

½ cup soy sauce

¼ cup honey

2 tablespoons hoisin sauce

2 tablespoons rice vinegar

2 tablespoons Shaoxing wine

2 tablespoons sesame seeds, for garnish

Fresh cilantro, for garnish

1 Place the ribs in one layer in a shallow dish. Mix together the garlic, soy sauce, honey, hoisin, vinegar, and Shaoxing wine and pour over the ribs, coating well. Reserve the unused marinade for basting. Cover and refrigerate for at least 6 hours.

2 Preheat the oven or grill to 350°F.

3 Transfer the ribs and marinade to a roasting pan and cook until brown and tender, about 35 to 45 minutes; brush with unused marinade from time to time and turn the ribs once or twice.

4 Remove the ribs and let stand briefly before garnishing with a sprinkle of sesame seeds and some cilantro.

ROSEMARY SPARERIBS

YIELDS: 4 Servings   **ACTIVE TIME:** 30 Minutes   **TOTAL TIME:** 4 Hours and 30 Minutes

The woodsy, lemon-pine flavor of rosemary goes perfectly with the ribs in this preparation.

INGREDIENTS

4½ lbs. pork spareribs, trimmed

3 garlic cloves, minced

½ cup olive oil

Salt and pepper, to taste

4 sprigs fresh rosemary,
plus more for garnish

1. Separate the ribs into individual servings (3 to 4 ribs per serving) and place in a large roasting pan.

2. In a small bowl, mix the garlic, olive oil, salt, and pepper. Pour the marinade over ribs, coating the ribs completely. Lay the rosemary sprigs on the meat.

3. Cover and refrigerate for at least 2 hours, preferably longer.

4. When ready to cook, preheat a gas or charcoal grill to 325°F. Discard the rosemary sprigs, place the ribs on the grill, and cook for 2 hours, or until the meat is tender.

5. Remove from the grill and let rest under aluminum foil for 10 minutes before garnishing with additional rosemary.

SESAME-CRUSTED PORK RIBS

YIELDS: 4 Servings **ACTIVE TIME:** 30 Minutes **TOTAL TIME:** 3 Hours and 30 Minutes

Sweet pineapple plays well here with the nuttiness of sesame seeds.

INGREDIENTS

2 tablespoons unsalted butter

1 small pineapple, peeled, cored, and diced

1 cup low-sodium soy sauce

½ cup bourbon

½ cup ketchup

3 tablespoons apple cider vinegar

¼ cup packed brown sugar

1 tablespoon red pepper flakes

2 garlic cloves, chopped

1 tablespoon peeled and grated ginger

3 lbs. baby back pork ribs, trimmed

2 tablespoons toasted sesame oil

Salt and pepper, to taste

¾ cup sesame seeds

---

1   Preheat the oven or grill to 300°F.

2   In a saucepan over medium heat, melt the butter and add the pineapple chunks, sautéing for 3 minutes.

3   Stir in the soy sauce, bourbon, ketchup, vinegar, sugar, red pepper flakes, garlic, and ginger. Bring to a gentle simmer and cook, stirring occasionally until thickened, about 20 minutes.

4   Pour the glaze into a blender and puree until smooth. Set aside.

5   Place the ribs on a roasting trivet set inside a large roasting pan and rub all over with the sesame oil. Season generously with salt and pepper.

6   Roast until the meat is tender and coming away from the bones, about 3 hours, basting with glaze during last 30 minutes of cooking.

7   Remove the ribs when ready and baste with any remaining glaze before generously sprinkling with sesame seeds. Preheat the broiler to high or the grill to 450°F.

8   Cook under the broiler or on the grill until the sesame seeds are browned, about 5 to 7 minutes.

9   Cut between the bones to separate before serving.

NOT YOUR AVERAGE BOURBON COCKTAILS

Hints of sesame and mole in your cocktail? It works for ribs, and it works for these.

PASSING DEADLINE

1½ oz. bourbon

½ oz. Cocchi Storico Vermouth di Torino

½ oz. Lustau East India Solera Sherry

½ oz. Salers Gentiane

1 spoonful of turbinado syrup

Dash of Angostura Bitters

Dash of Bittermens Xocolatl Mole Bitters

Dusting of cinnamon, for garnish

1 cinnamon stick, for garnish

1 Place all of the cocktail ingredients in a mixing glass filled with ice and stir until chilled. Strain into a rocks glass filled with ice and garnish with a dusting of cinnamon and the cinnamon stick.

A DARK ART

½ oz. black sesame syrup

1½ oz. Maker's 46 bourbon

Juice of 1 lime

13 dashes Angostura bitters

Pinch of activated charcoal

1 jasmine blossom, for garnish (optional)

1 To make the black sesame syrup, place ½ cup of black sesame seeds in a skillet and toast for 1 to 2 minutes. Remove from the saucepan and set aside. Combine 3 cups sugar and 2 cups hot water and stir until dissolved. Place the sesame seeds and syrup in a blender or food processor and puree for 1 to 2 minutes. Let the mixture sit for 3 to 12 hours and then strain it through 2 to 3 layers of cheesecloth while squeezing the mixture to remove all the liquid. Discard the solids, add 2 tablespoons of vodka and ½ teaspoon of orange blossom water, stir, and transfer the syrup to an airtight container. The syrup will keep for approximately 2 weeks.

2 Combine the cocktail ingredients in a cocktail shaker filled with ice and shake vigorously. Strain into a coupe containing ice and, if using, garnish with the jasmine blossom.

SPICY OYSTER SAUCE PORK RIBS

YIELDS: 4 Servings   **ACTIVE TIME:** 25 Minutes   **TOTAL TIME:** 5 Hours and 40 Minutes

If you're not a fan of oysters, don't be put off by oyster sauce. Yes, it is made from caramelized oyster juice, but this flavor enhancer isn't fishy or briny. It has a sweet-and-savory tang that evokes soy sauce and barbecue sauce, which is why it works so well in this recipe.

INGREDIENTS

2 garlic cloves, minced

1 tablespoon peeled and minced fresh ginger

Juice of 1 lime

⅓ cup oyster sauce

¼ cup soy sauce

1 teaspoon red pepper flakes

1 teaspoon ground cumin

½ teaspoon ground coriander

3 tablespoons brown sugar

2 tablespoons olive oil

2 tablespoons sesame oil

3 tablespoons water

½ teaspoon kosher salt

¼ teaspoon black pepper

4 lbs. pork spareribs, trimmed and separated

3 scallions, sliced, for garnish

1 red chile pepper, seeded and sliced thin, for garnish

1 small bunch fresh cilantro, roughly chopped, for garnish

1 lime, cut into wedges, for garnish

1 In a shallow dish, mix together all the ingredients, apart from the ribs and garnishes. Place the ribs in the resulting marinade, reserving some for later. Turn the ribs to coat. Cover and refrigerate for 4 hours.

2 When ready to cook the ribs, remove them from the fridge and preheat a gas or charcoal grill to 325°F.

3 Cook the ribs until they are tender and nicely browned, turning a few times, about 1 hour; basting with the reserved marinade from time to time.

4 To serve, arrange the ribs on a serving platter and garnish with the scallions, chile, and cilantro. Serve with the lime wedges on the side.

ASIAN SPARERIBS

YIELDS: 4 Servings **ACTIVE TIME:** 20 Minutes **TOTAL TIME:** 24 Hours

St. Louis-style spareribs are ideal for this recipe that features a spicy and flowery depth of flavor.

INGREDIENTS

¾ cup hoisin sauce

⅓ cup dark soy sauce

3 tablespoons brown sugar

3 tablespoons honey

1 tablespoon sesame oil

1 tablespoon Chinese five-spice powder

1 teaspoon onion powder

1 teaspoon garlic powder

1 teaspoon ground ginger

1 (4-lb.) rack pork spareribs, cleaned and trimmed

1. Whisk together everything apart from the ribs in a mixing bowl until the brown sugar and honey have dissolved.

2. Place the ribs in a large resealable bag; if too large, cut the rack in half and place in two separate bags.

3. Pour about two-thirds of the sauce into the bag(s), removing any excess air before sealing and chilling overnight. Cover and reserve remaining sauce.

4. The next day, preheat the oven or grill to 275°F. Line a large roasting pan with aluminum foil and sit a large roasting trivet on top.

5. Remove the ribs from the bag(s) and arrange on the trivet. Roast until the ribs are very tender, about 2½ hours, basting with the reserved sauce from time to time.

6. Remove the ribs and let rest under aluminum foil for 10 minutes. Preheat the broiler to high or the grill to 450°F.

7. Caramelize the ribs under the broiler or on the grill, turning once, for about 6 to 8 minutes in total.

8. Remove the ribs and let cool briefly before cutting and serving.

HOISIN SPARERIBS

YIELDS: 4 Servings   **ACTIVE TIME:** 20 Minutes   **TOTAL TIME:** 24 Hours

Don't let unfamiliar ingredients deter you. When this sauce caramelizes all you'll be thinking about is the how amazing these ribs taste.

INGREDIENTS

1 (3-lb.) rack pork spareribs, trimmed

2 cups granulated sugar

⅔ cup ketchup

¼ cup Shaoxing wine

¼ cup dark soy sauce

¼ cup hoisin sauce

1 tablespoon kosher salt

1 teaspoon white pepper

1 teaspoon Chinese five-spice powder

1 teaspoon ground ginger

1 handful fresh cilantro, torn, for garnish

1 Place the ribs in a large resealable bag; if too large, cut the rack in half and place in two separate bags.

2 In a mixing bowl, whisk together the remaining ingredients, apart from cilantro, until a gritty sauce forms.

3 Pour about half of the sauce into the bag(s), removing any excess air before sealing and refrigerating overnight. Cover and reserve the remaining sauce.

4 The next day, preheat the oven or grill to 300°F. Line a large roasting pan with aluminum foil and sit a large roasting trivet on top.

5 Remove the ribs from the bag(s) and arrange on trivet. Roast until the meat is very tender, about 2½ hours, basting with the reserved sauce from time to time.

6 Remove the ribs when ready and let rest under aluminum foil for at least 10 minutes. Preheat the broiler to high or the grill to 450°F.

7 Cut between the bones to separate the ribs. Broil until lightly charred and caramelized, turning once halfway through, about 6 to 8 minutes in total.

8 Transfer the ribs to a platter and garnish with the cilantro.

BALSAMIC PORK RIBS

YIELDS: 4 Servings   **ACTIVE TIME:** 20 Minutes   **TOTAL TIME:** 24 Hours

The sharpness of the balsamic cuts through the naturally sweet flavor of the pork to incredible effect.

INGREDIENTS

For the Ribs

6 garlic cloves, minced

3 tablespoons brown sugar

3 tablespoons balsamic vinegar

½ teaspoon cayenne pepper

1 tablespoon kosher salt

1 teaspoon black pepper

4 lbs. pork spareribs, cleaned and trimmed

½ cup water

For the Glaze

½ cup balsamic vinegar

1 cup hot water

¼ cup packed brown sugar

¼ cup ketchup

1 tablespoon molasses

½ teaspoon mustard powder

1   To begin preparations for the ribs, stir together the garlic, sugar, vinegar, cayenne, salt, and black pepper in a small mixing bowl.

2   Rub the marinade into both sides of the ribs. Place the ribs in a large roasting pan and cover the dish with aluminum foil. Refrigerate overnight.

3   The next day, preheat the oven or grill to 425°F. Pour water into the pan around the ribs and cover with foil.

4   Roast until the ribs are tender, about 2 hours. Remove and transfer the ribs to a platter.

5   To begin preparations for the glaze, add all of the ingredients and any juices from the roasting pan to a small saucepan. Whisk to combine.

6   Bring the glaze to a boil over medium heat, whisking from time to time. Cook until the glaze has reduced and thickened, about 8 to 10 minutes.

7   Preheat the broiler to high or the grill to 450°F. Brush the ribs with glaze and cook until browned and sticky, turning once, about 6 to 8 minutes in total.

8   Transfer the ribs to a platter and cut into serving portions. Serve with the remaining glaze on side.

RUBS

All the recipes in this book are great, but once you have familiarized yourself with the fundamentals of cooking ribs, you can conjure up your own recipes, creating flavor profiles that best suit your palate and preparing the ribs exactly how you like them. The following rub recipes work on any type of ribs.

CAJUN RUB

YIELD: About ¾ Cup **ACTIVE TIME:** 5 Minutes **TOTAL TIME:** 5 Minutes

INGREDIENTS

¼ cup kosher salt

2 tablespoons black pepper

2 teaspoons paprika

2 teaspoons garlic powder

1 teaspoon onion powder

1 teaspoon cayenne pepper

1 teaspoon dried thyme

1 Using a spoon, combine all of the ingredients in a small bowl and mix thoroughly. Apply to meat when finished or store in an airtight container for up to 1 month.

CHINESE FIVE-SPICE RUB

YIELD: ½ Cup **ACTIVE TIME:** 5 Minutes **TOTAL TIME:** 5 Minutes

INGREDIENTS

1 tablespoon ground star anise

1 tablespoon cinnamon

1 tablespoon ground Sichuan peppercorn

1 tablespoon ground fennel

1 tablespoon ground cloves

1 tablespoon garlic powder

1 tablespoon ground ginger

1 tablespoon kosher salt

1 Using a spoon, combine all of the ingredients in a small bowl and mix thoroughly. Apply to meat when finished or store in an airtight container for up to 1 month.

COFFEE RUB

YIELD: 1 Cup **ACTIVE TIME:** 5 Minutes **TOTAL TIME:** 5 Minutes

INGREDIENTS

¼ cup ground coffee

2 tablespoons dark brown sugar

2 tablespoons cayenne pepper

2 tablespoons garlic powder

2 tablespoons paprika

2 tablespoons onion powder

1 tablespoon ground cumin

1 tablespoon kosher salt

1 Using a spoon, combine all of the ingredients in a small bowl and mix thoroughly. Apply to meat when finished or store in an airtight container for up to 1 month.

HOT & SPICY CHILI RUB

YIELD: About ½ Cup **ACTIVE TIME:** 5 Minutes **TOTAL TIME:** 5 Minutes

INGREDIENTS

3 tablespoons chili powder

3 tablespoons smoked paprika

1 tablespoon dried oregano

2 teaspoons ground cumin

2 teaspoons black pepper

2 teaspoons kosher salt

1 teaspoon dried thyme

1 In a small bowl, thoroughly combine all the ingredients for the rub. Apply to meat when finished or store in an airtight container for up to 1 month.

OREGANO-GARLIC RUB

YIELD: About ¼ Cup **ACTIVE TIME:** 5 Minutes **TOTAL TIME:** 5 Minutes

INGREDIENTS

1 tablespoon finely chopped fresh oregano

2 garlic cloves, minced

2 sprigs fresh thyme, leaves removed

2 teaspoons black pepper

1 teaspoon kosher salt

1 teaspoon ground cumin

1 teaspoon ground coriander

1 In a small bowl, thoroughly combine all the ingredients for the rub. Apply to meat when finished.

SMOKED PAPRIKA RUB

YIELD: ½ Cup **ACTIVE TIME:** 5 Minutes **TOTAL TIME:** 5 Minutes

INGREDIENTS

2 tablespoons smoked paprika

2 teaspoons ground coriander

2 teaspoons ground cumin

1 teaspoon cayenne pepper

1 tablespoon black pepper

1 tablespoon kosher salt

1 In a small bowl, thoroughly combine all the ingredients for the rub. Apply to meat when finished or store in an airtight container for up to 1 month.

SOUTHWESTERN DRY RUB

YIELD: About 3 Tablespoons **ACTIVE TIME:** 5 Minutes **TOTAL TIME:** 5 Minutes

INGREDIENTS

2 teaspoons chili powder

2 teaspoons paprika

1 teaspoon cayenne pepper

1 teaspoon ground cumin

1 teaspoon ground coriander

1 teaspoon minced garlic

1 teaspoon kosher salt

1 teaspoon black pepper

1 Using a spoon, combine all of the ingredients in a small bowl and mix thoroughly. Apply to meat when finished.

ST. LOUIS RUB

YIELD: About 1 Cup **ACTIVE TIME:** 5 Minutes **TOTAL TIME:** 5 Minutes

INGREDIENTS

¼ cup paprika

3 tablespoons garlic powder

2 tablespoons black pepper

2 tablespoons kosher salt

2 tablespoons onion powder

1 tablespoon dark brown sugar

1 tablespoon ground ginger

1 tablespoon mustard powder

1 teaspoon celery salt

1 Using a spoon, combine all of the ingredients in a small bowl and mix thoroughly. Apply to meat when finished or store in an airtight container for up to 1 month.

BEEF & LAMB RIBS

BEEF AND LAMB both bring their own unique flavors to the grill, with the juicy richness of beef lending itself to almost any flavor combination, while the savory, nearly overpowering taste of lamb begs for a sharp dash of citrus or a refreshing mint sauce to bring the dish full circle. These recipes highlight the best of both proteins, proving that they each desserve a hallowed place in the barbecue hall of fame.

BEEF RIBS WITH BOURBON BBQ SAUCE

YIELDS: 4 Servings **ACTIVE TIME:** 1 Hour **TOTAL TIME:** 24 Hours

Beef ribs aren't as fatty as their pork counterparts, but cooked properly they are just as tender and delicious.

INGREDIENTS

For the Ribs

2 tablespoons brown sugar

2 teaspoons kosher salt

2 teaspoons smoked paprika

1 teaspoon black pepper

½ teaspoon mustard powder

1 pinch cayenne pepper

5 lbs. beef short ribs, cleaned and trimmed

4 cups beef stock (for homemade, see page 274)

For the Sauce

¾ cup brown sugar

1 cup ketchup

¼ cup red wine vinegar or apple cider vinegar

1 tablespoon water

1 tablespoon bourbon

1 teaspoon tomato paste

1 teaspoon Worcestershire sauce

1 tablespoon mustard powder

1 teaspoon paprika

1 teaspoon kosher salt

½ teaspoon black pepper

1. To begin preparations for the ribs, stir together the sugar, salt, paprika, black pepper, mustard powder, and cayenne in a mixing bowl.

2. Rub the spice mix into both sides of the ribs. Divide the ribs between two large roasting pans, covering them with aluminum foil. Refrigerate overnight.

3. The next day, preheat the oven or grill to 325°F. Pour 2 cups stock into each pan around the ribs and recover with foil.

4. Braise the ribs in the oven or on the grill until the beef is very tender, about 3 hours. When ready, transfer the ribs to platters and cover loosely with aluminum foil. Preheat the broiler to high or the grill to 450°F.

5. To begin preparations for the sauce, combine all ingredients in a small saucepan. Bring to a simmer, whisking until the sugar dissolves.

6. Let the sauce simmer until slightly thickened, about 3 to 5 minutes. Remove from heat and let cool for 10 minutes.

7. Brush some sauce onto the ribs. Place the ribs under the broiler or on the grill, cooking until caramelized and lightly charred, turning once, about 6 to 8 minutes. Be sure to baste with more sauce from time to time.

8. Transfer the ribs to a platter and cut into individual ribs before serving.

BOURBON-GLAZED BEEF SHORT RIBS

YIELDS: 4 Servings   **ACTIVE TIME:** 20 Minutes   **TOTAL TIME:** 24 Hours

Look for beef short rib racks, rather than whole ribs, for best results.

INGREDIENTS

For the Ribs

¼ cup bourbon

2 tablespoons brown sugar

2 teaspoons kosher salt

2 teaspoons smoked paprika

1 teaspoon black pepper

1 pinch cayenne pepper

5 lbs. beef short ribs, trimmed

4 cups beef stock (for homemade, see page 274))

For the Glaze

1 cup beef stock (for homemade, see page 274)

¼ cup brown sugar

¼ cup bourbon

1. To begin preparations for the ribs, in a mixing bowl, combine the bourbon, sugar, salt, paprika, black pepper, and cayenne.

2. Rub the marinade into both sides of the ribs. Divide the ribs between two large roasting pans, covering them with aluminum foil. Chill overnight.

3. The next day, preheat the oven or grill to 325°F. Pour 2 cups broth into each pan around the ribs and cover with foil.

4. Braise in the oven or on the grill until the beef is very tender, about 2½ hours. When ready, transfer the ribs platters and cover loosely with aluminum foil. Preheat the broiler to high or the grill to 450°F.

5. To prepare the glaze, whisk the ingredients together in a small saucepan. Bring to the boil over medium heat and cook until reduced by half, about 10 minutes.

6. Brush some glaze onto the ribs. Place the ribs under the broiler or on the grill, broiling until caramelized and lightly charred, while turning once, 6 to 8 minutes. Be sure to baste with more glaze from time to time.

7. Transfer the ribs to a platter and cut the racks into individual ribs before serving.

GRILLED BEEF RIBS

YIELDS: 4 Servings **ACTIVE TIME:** 20 Minutes **TOTAL TIME:** 1 Hour and 30 Minutes

Boiling the ribs first helps jump start the cooking process.

INGREDIENTS

5 lbs. beef whole ribs, trimmed and separated

2 red chile peppers, diced

1 onion, diced

2 garlic cloves, roughly chopped

¼ cup honey

1 teaspoon kosher salt

½ teaspoon black pepper

¼ cup tomato paste

2 tablespoons white wine vinegar

1 dash Tabasco™

¾ cup water

Canola oil, for brushing

1 Place the ribs in a stockpot of boiling water and reduce to a simmer for 20 minutes. Drain and pat dry with paper towels.

2 In a saucepan, mix together the chile peppers, onion, garlic, honey, salt, black pepper, tomato paste, vinegar, and Tabasco™. Whisk in the water and bring to a boil. Cook for 10 minutes until reduced and thickened. Remove from heat and let cool.

3 Preheat a gas or charcoal grill to 350°F.

4 Brush the ribs with oil and grill for 20 minutes, turning once and occasionally basting with the prepared sauce.

5 Remove the ribs from the grill and let rest under aluminum foil for 10 minutes before serving.

GRILLED BOURBON
SHORT RIBS
WITH ONIONS

YIELDS: 4 Servings   **ACTIVE TIME:** 30 Minutes   **TOTAL TIME:** 3 Hours

This is a homey dish that tastes especially good when autumn arrives. Don't skip the onions—when grilled and flavored with the sauce they take on a wonderful charred sweetness.

INGREDIENTS

½ cup packed brown sugar

½ cup soy sauce

¼ cup bourbon

¼ cup olive oil

3 garlic cloves, minced

2 tablespoons peeled and grated fresh ginger

4 lbs. beef short ribs, trimmed and separated

2 large sweet onions, sliced into ½-inch rounds and speared with toothpicks

1   In a mixing bowl, combine the sugar, soy sauce, bourbon, olive oil, garlic, and ginger. Place the ribs in a large resealable plastic bag.

2   Pour two-thirds of the marinade over the ribs and securely seal the bag, removing any excess air. Turn the bag over several times to completely coat the ribs. Refrigerate for at least 2 hours, preferably longer. Cover and refrigerate the remaining marinade.

3   When ready to cook the ribs, preheat a gas or charcoal grill to 375°F.

4   Remove the ribs from the marinade and place on the grill, grilling for 15 to 20 minutes until tender and cooked through, turning halfway through and brushing with the reserved marinade from time to time.

5   Remove the ribs from the grill and let rest under aluminum foil.

6   Place the onions on the and cook until lightly charred, brushing with marinade from time to time, about 7 to 10 minutes.

7   Remove the onions from the grill, transfer to a platter, and remove the toothpicks before arranging the ribs on top and serving.

CARIBBEAN BEEF RIBS

YIELDS: 4 Servings **ACTIVE TIME:** 30 Minutes **TOTAL TIME:** 24 Hours

The pungent sweet and smoky spices in this dry rub impart an island flair that is enlivened when you finish off these ribs with a healthy squeeze of lime juice.

INGREDIENTS

2 tablespoons brown sugar

2 tablespoons onion powder

2 tablespoons garlic powder

1 tablespoon kosher salt

1 tablespoon smoked paprika or regular paprika

2 teaspoons cayenne pepper

2 teaspoons ground allspice

2 teaspoons black pepper

1 teaspoon red pepper flakes

1 teaspoon ground cumin

1 teaspoon ground nutmeg

1 teaspoon cinnamon

1 teaspoon dried thyme

1 (4-lb.) rack whole beef ribs, trimmed

2 limes, halved, for serving

1 Stir together all ingredients, apart from the ribs and limes, in a small bowl.

2 Rub the seasoning mix into both sides of the ribs. Place the ribs on a roasting trivet set inside a large roasting pan lined with aluminum foil. Cover and refrigerate overnight.

3 The next day, preheat an oven or grill to 275°F.

4 Roast the ribs very tender, about 6 hours. The ribs are done when the meat is falling away from the bones.

5 Remove the ribs from the oven or grill and let rest under aluminum foil for 10 minutes.

6 Cut between the bones into the ribs and arrange on a dish, serving with the lime halves.

GRILLED SESAME SEED BEEF RIBS

YIELDS: 4 Servings **ACTIVE TIME:** 20 Minutes **TOTAL TIME:** 6 Hours and 30 Minutes

Whole ribs are longer and thinner compared to short ribs, although the latter would also work in this recipe.

INGREDIENTS

1 (3-lb.) rack beef whole ribs, trimmed

1 cup hoisin sauce

2 tablespoons honey

1 tablespoon rice vinegar

½ teaspoon kosher salt

½ teaspoon black pepper

2 tablespoons sesame seeds, for garnish

2 scallions, sliced thin, for garnish

2 red chile peppers, seeded and sliced thin, for garnish

1 handful fresh cilantro, torn, for garnish

1 lemon, cut into wedges, for serving

1 Preheat an oven or grill to 275°F.

2 In a mixing bowl, stir together the hoisin sauce, honey, vinegar, salt, and pepper. Rub about half of the sauce all over the ribs and then place them on a roasting trivet set inside a large roasting dish lined with aluminum foil.

3 Roast the ribs until very tender, between 5 and 6 hours, basting from time to time with the remaining sauce. When ready, the meat should be falling away from the bones.

4 Remove the ribs from the oven or grill and let rest under aluminum foil for 10 minutes.

5 Cut between bones into ribs and arrange in a serving dish. Garnish with the sesame seeds, scallions, chile peppers, and cilantro, and serve with the lemon wedges.

KALBI

YIELDS: 4 Servings   **ACTIVE TIME:** 30 Minutes   **TOTAL TIME:** 5 Hours

Korean-style short ribs can be sourced from most good Asian markets. They may also be labeled as flanken ribs; these ribs are easy to identify as they are butchered across the rib bones, meaning each slice has a few pieces of bone. The sweet-and-savory marinade is elevated by the gochujang, a fermented spice paste, making for tender and tasty beef.

INGREDIENTS

5 lbs. Korean-style beef short ribs

1 cup brown sugar

1 cup soy sauce

⅓ cup water

⅓ cup mirin

2 tablespoons gochujang

1 small onion, grated

5 garlic cloves, minced

1 tablespoon peeled and minced fresh ginger

1½ tablespoons toasted sesame oil

1. Place the ribs on a large cutting board and sprinkle with sugar, rubbing the sugar into ribs. Let stand at room temperature for 10 minutes.

2. In a mixing bowl, whisk together the remaining ingredients.

3. Transfer the ribs to a large, shallow dish and cover with the marinade, turning ribs to coat. Cover and refrigerate for at least 4 hours, preferably longer, turning the ribs over every 2 hours.

4. When ready to cook, preheat a gas or charcoal grill to 400°F; if using charcoals, wait until they are covered in ash.

5. Remove the ribs from the marinade, wiping off any excess with paper towels. Lay the ribs on the grill, cooking until charred and browned all over, turning once, about 6 to 8 minutes in total.

6. Remove the ribs from the grill and let rest under aluminum foil for 10 minutes before slicing and serving.

CHURRASCO RIBS
WITH FAROFA

YIELDS: 4 Servings **ACTIVE TIME:** 30 Minutes **TOTAL TIME:** 7 Hours

In Brazil, the Portuguese word *churrasco* refers to both grilled beef and meat in general. *Farofa* is a staple side dish with grilled meat; its foundation is coarse manioc flour, also known as cassava flour or tapioca flour, which is then seasoned with everything from scallions and olives to raisins.

INGREDIENTS

For the Ribs

1 (3-lb.) rack beef whole ribs, trimmed

2 tablespoons kosher salt

1 tablespoon black pepper

1 cup beef stock (for homemade, see page 274)

For the Farofa

2 tablespoons unsalted butter

2 cups manioc flour

Salt and pepper, to taste

2 scallions, green tops only, sliced, for garnish

1 handful fresh parsley, torn, for garnish

1 Preheat an oven or grill to 275°F.

2 To begin preparations for the ribs, rub both sides of the ribs with salt and black pepper. Place on a roasting trivet set inside a large roasting pan lined with aluminum foil.

3 Roast the ribs until very tender, about 6 hours, basting from time to time with the beef stock. When the ribs are ready, the meat should be falling away from the bones.

4 To begin preparations for the *farofa*, melt the butter in a saucepan set over medium heat. Add the manioc flour, toasting in the butter until golden and fragrant, about 3 to 4 minutes.

5 Remove the *farofa* from heat and season to taste with salt and pepper. Cover and set aside until ready to serve.

6 When ready, remove the ribs from oven or grill. Let rest under aluminum foil for 10 minutes. Garnish the *farofa* with the scallions and parsley and serve alongside the ribs.

DRINKS TO COOK BY

No matter your preferred method, cooking ribs requires some time and attention. These cocktails are light and refreshing enough to go down easy and not leave you feeling stuffed, because there's plenty of food on the way.

MAKER'S MULE

1½ parts Maker's Mark bourbon

Splash of lime juice

Ginger beer, chilled, to top

1 lime wedge, for garnish

1 Place the bourbon and lime juice in a highball glass filled with ice. Top with the ginger beer and garnish with the lime wedge.

STREETCAR NAMED DESIRE

1½ oz. bourbon

¾ oz. Cocktail & Sons Mint and Lemon Verbena syrup

¾ oz. lemon juice

4 dashes of Angostura Bitters

1 sprig fresh mint, for garnish

1 Place all of the cocktail ingredients, except for the bitters, in a cocktail shaker filled with ice and shake vigorously. Strain into a rocks glass filled with ice, top with the bitters, and garnish with the mint sprig.

OLD TIMER

1½ oz. bourbon

½ oz. Cynar

½ oz. Punt e Mes vermouth

½ oz. lemon juice

¼ oz. simple syrup

2 to 4 dashes of Angostura Bitters

Club soda, to top

1 orange twist, for garnish

1 Place all of the cocktail ingredients, except for the club soda, in a cocktail shaker filled with ice and shake vigorously. Double-strain into a Collins glass filled with ice, top with soda, and garnish with the orange twist.

BBQ LAMB RIBS

YIELDS: 4 Servings **ACTIVE TIME:** 1 Hour **TOTAL TIME:** 24 Hours

Lamb is often thought of being "gamy" but when cooked with this sweet sauce no one will be able to make that claim.

INGREDIENTS

2 sprigs fresh rosemary

2 garlic cloves, crushed

1 cup distilled white vinegar

¾ cup ketchup

2 teaspoons honey

1 teaspoon Worcestershire sauce

¾ cup dark brown sugar

1 tablespoon chili powder

1½ teaspoons kosher salt

1 teaspoon black pepper

2 (3-lb.) racks lamb ribs, trimmed

1   Combine all ingredients, except for the ribs, in a saucepan.

2   Bring to a boil over a high heat before reducing to a simmer; cook until thickened, about 20 to 30 minutes. Set aside to cool for 30 minutes.

3   Place the ribs on a roasting trivet set inside a large roasting pan lined with aluminum foil. Brush half the sauce onto the ribs, reserving the other half. Cover with aluminum foil and refrigerate overnight.

4   The next day, preheat a gas or charcoal grill to 250°F; if using charcoal, bank coals on one side of grill. Place the ribs on the grill and cook until dark brown and tender, about 3 hours, basting with the reserved barbecue sauce from time to time.

5   When the meat is tender and falling off the bone, remove the ribs from heat and let rest under aluminum foil for 10 minutes.

6   Cut between the bones to separate the ribs before serving.

GRILLED LAMB RIBS

YIELDS: 4 Servings **ACTIVE TIME:** 45 Minutes **TOTAL TIME:** 3 Hours and 30 Minutes

Coffee grounds add both a floral and flavorful note to this recipe that is sure to perk up your taste buds.

INGREDIENTS

For the Ribs

2 tablespoons kosher salt

2 tablespoons brown sugar

2 tablespoons coffee grounds, ground to a fine powder

1 teaspoon black pepper

1 teaspoon mustard powder

1 (4-lb.) rack lamb ribs, cleaned and trimmed

For the Mop Sauce

2 cups apple cider vinegar

½ teaspoon kosher salt

2 tablespoons molasses

½ teaspoon black pepper

1 pinch cayenne pepper

1 pinch red pepper flakes

1. To begin preparations for the ribs, combine the salt, sugar, coffee, black pepper, and mustard powder in a small bowl.

2. Rub the seasoning mix into the ribs and let them sit at room temperature for 1 hour.

3. To prepare the mop sauce, in a mixing bowl, whisk together all of the ingredients until the molasses dissolves.

4. Preheat a gas or charcoal grill to 325°F. Make sure to bank coals to one side if using a charcoal grill. Place the ribs on the grill and cook, turning once, until browned, about 12 to 15 minutes total.

5. Reduce the temperature to 250°F or move the ribs away from the coals on a charcoal grill, and grill until tender, turning and basting with mop sauce every 10 to 15 minutes, for about 1½ hours.

6. When the ribs are tender and the meat is falling away from the bones, remove and let rest under aluminum foil for 10 minutes.

7. Pour any unused mop sauce into a saucepan and bring to a boil over a high heat, cooking until slightly reduced, about 2 to 4 minutes.

8. Cut between the bones to separate the ribs, brushing with reduced mop sauce and serving with the remainder on the side.

CHARGRILLED LAMB RIBS
WITH CORIANDER & PEPPER

YIELDS: 4 Servings **ACTIVE TIME:** 30 Minutes **TOTAL TIME:** 3 Hours

Coriander seeds are subtly aromatic, lending themselves well to the grassy quality of lamb.

INGREDIENTS

3 tablespoons coriander seeds, lightly crushed

1 tablespoon kosher salt

2 teaspoons red pepper flakes

2 teaspoons black pepper

1 pinch cayenne pepper

1 (4-lb.) rack lamb ribs, cleaned and trimmed

1 cup apple cider vinegar

3 tablespoons brown sugar

2 tablespoons olive oil

1 Stir together the coriander, salt, red pepper flakes, black pepper, and cayenne. Rub about two-thirds into ribs and let sit at room temperature for 1 hour.

2 Whisk the vinegar, sugar, and olive oil into the remaining spice mix. Cover and set aside.

3 Preheat a gas or charcoal grill to 325°F. Make sure to bank coals to one side if using a charcoal grill. Place the ribs on the grill and cook, turning once, until browned, about 10 minutes.

4 Reduce temperature to 250°F, or move the ribs away from the coals on a charcoal grill, and grill until tender, about 1½ hours, turning and basting with prepared sauce every 10 to 15 minutes.

5 Remove the ribs and let rest under aluminum foil for 10 minutes before cutting into individual ribs and serving.

CHILE-VINEGAR LAMB RIBS

YIELDS: 4 Servings **ACTIVE TIME:** 1 Hour **TOTAL TIME:** 7 Hours

Lamb is used widely in parts of China and Mongolia, making the ingredients in this recipe a natural fit.

INGREDIENTS

2 tablespoons fennel seeds, lightly toasted

2 tablespoons sesame seeds

1½ teaspoons red pepper flakes

1 tablespoon flaked sea salt

2 teaspoons black peppercorns, lightly crushed

1 (4-lb.) rack lamb ribs, trimmed

¾ cups dark soy sauce

1 cup rice vinegar

2 teaspoons granulated sugar

3 red Thai chile peppers, finely chopped

2 scallions, greens only, sliced, for garnish

1 In a mixing bowl, stir together the fennel seeds, sesame seeds, red pepper flakes, sea salt, and peppercorns.

2 Rub about half the spice mixture onto the meat side of the ribs. Set the ribs on a roasting trivet set inside a large roasting pan lined with aluminum foil. Cover and refrigerate for at least 4 hours, preferably longer.

3 When ready to cook, preheat a gas or charcoal grill to 325°F. Make sure to bank coals to one side if using a charcoal grill. Place the ribs on the grill and cook, turning once, until browned, about 10 minutes.

4 In the meantime, stir together the soy sauce, vinegar, sugar, and chiles in a small bowl until the sugar dissolves. Divide the chile-vinegar between two bowls.

5 Reduce the grill temperature to 250°F, or move the ribs away from the coals on a charcoal grill, and continue grilling until the ribs are tender, turning and basting with chile-vinegar from one bowl every 10 to 15 minutes. The ribs should be ready in about 1 hour and 45 minutes.

6 When ready, places the ribs on a platter and let rest under aluminum foil for 10 minutes. Cut between the bones to separate them.

7 Sprinkle the remaining spice mixture and the scallions over the ribs and serve with the reserved bowl of chile-vinegar.

SPICY LAMB RIBS
WITH TZATZIKI & LEMON

YIELDS: 4 Servings   **ACTIVE TIME:** 30 Minutes   **TOTAL TIME:** 3 Hours

Transport yourself to a Greek island village with these assertively spiced ribs.

INGREDIENTS

2 tablespoons kosher salt

2 tablespoons brown sugar

1 tablespoon freshly ground cumin,

1 tablespoon freshly ground coriander

½ teaspoon black pepper

1 (4-lb.) rack lamb ribs, cleaned and trimmed

⅔ cup apple cider vinegar

Tzatziki, for serving

Olive oil, for serving

1 handful fresh parsley, for serving

Lemon wedges, for serving

1. Stir together the salt, sugar, cumin, coriander, and black pepper in a small bowl. Rub half of the mixture into the ribs and let them sit at room temperature for 1 hour.

2. Whisk the vinegar into the remaining spice mix. Cover and set aside.

3. Preheat a gas or charcoal grill to 325°F. Make sure to bank coals to one side if using a charcoal grill. Place the ribs on the grill and cook, turning once, until browned, about 10 minutes.

4. Reduce the temperature to 250°F, or move the ribs away from the coals on a charcoal grill, and grill until tender, about 1½ hours, turning and basting with prepared sauce every 10 to 15 minutes.

5. Remove the ribs and let rest under aluminum foil for 10 minutes. Cut into individual ribs. Place the tzatziki in a bowl, drizzle with olive oil, and sprinkle the parsley on top. Serve alongside the ribs and lemon wedges.

YUZU SESAME LAMB RIBS

YIELDS: 4 Servings **ACTIVE TIME:** 1 Hour **TOTAL TIME:** 4 Hours

Yuzu is a fragrant and tart citrus fruit that is the base of this Japanese-style *yakiniku* sauce.

INGREDIENTS

For the Ribs

1 tablespoon kosher salt

1 tablespoon granulated sugar

1 teaspoon black pepper

1 teaspoon Chinese five-spice powder

1 (4-lb.) rack lamb ribs, trimmed

For the Yakiniku Sauce

1 garlic clove, chopped

½ cup yuzu juice

⅓ cup soy sauce

3 tablespoons mirin

3 tablespoons granulated sugar

2 teaspoons honey

2 teaspoons sesame oil

1 tablespoon cornstarch, mixed to a slurry with 1 tablespoon water

2 teaspoons sesame seeds, toasted and ground

1   To begin preparations for the ribs, stir together the salt, sugar, black pepper, and five-spice powder in a small bowl. Rub mixture into the ribs and let them sit at room temperature for 1 hour.

2   To begin preparations for the sauce, in a saucepan, combine everything for sauce, apart from cornstarch slurry and ground sesame seeds. Bring to a boil over medium heat and then reduce to a simmer until slightly thickened, about 5 minutes.

3   Strain the sauce into a small saucepan and return to a simmer. Whisk in the cornstarch slurry and ground sesame seeds, returning to a simmer until the sauce has thickened. Remove from heat and cover until ready to use.

4   Preheat a gas or charcoal grill to 325°F. Make sure to bank coals to one side if using a charcoal grill. Place the ribs on the grill and cook, turning once, until browned, about 10 minutes total.

5   Reduce temperature to 250°F, or move the ribs away from the coals on a charcoal grill, and cook until tender, about 1 hour and 45 minutes, turning and basting with prepared sauce every 10 to 15 minutes.

6   Remove the ribs and let rest under aluminum foil for 10 minutes. Cut the rack into double ribs and serve.

MARINADES & BASTING SAUCES

There is something undeniably special about the alchemy of heat slowly coaxing out the divine flavors of fat and meat seasoned with the bare essentials. But it's also pretty great when unexpected seasoning results in a new taste sensation. So here is a selection of flavor-enhancing marinades and sauces for you to experiment with in your pursuit of the perfect ribs.

The same as with the rub recipes (see page 72), these can be plugged in to any ribs recipe in this book.

JAMAICAN JERK MARINADE

YIELD: About ¾ Cup **ACTIVE TIME:** 10 Minutes **TOTAL TIME:** 10 Minutes

INGREDIENTS

1 onion, minced

¼ cup scallions, minced

1 scotch bonnet pepper, chopped

3 tablespoons soy sauce

1 tablespoon white vinegar

3 tablespoons olive oil

2 teaspoons minced fresh thyme

2 teaspoons granulated sugar

1 teaspoon kosher salt

1 teaspoon black pepper

1 teaspoon ground allspice

½ teaspoon ground nutmeg

½ teaspoon cinnamon

1 Place all of the ingredients into a blender, and then pulse to the desired consistency. Remove and marinate meat immediately.

TIP: For a smokier flavor, consider adding 1 or 2 teaspoons of liquid smoke (like Colgin's) to the ingredients.

TANDOORI MARINADE

YIELD: 2¼ Cups **ACTIVE TIME:** 10 Minutes **TOTAL TIME:** 3 Hours

INGREDIENTS

2 tablespoons olive oil, plus more as needed

2 garlic cloves, minced

½ teaspoon ground turmeric

2 tablespoons ground cumin

1 tablespoon peeled and minced fresh ginger

1 teaspoon paprika

1 teaspoon coriander seeds

3 tablespoons minced fresh cilantro

Juice of ½ small lime

1½ cups plain yogurt

1 In a small skillet, heat the olive oil over medium heat. Add the remaining ingredients, except for the lime juice and yogurt, to the skillet and toast for 2 minutes. The spices, with the olive oil, should form a paste. If not, add more olive oil to the mixture.

2 Transfer the paste to a bowl and stir in the lime juice and yogurt. Place the meat in the marinade for at least 3 hours before grilling.

APPLE CIDER MARINADE

YIELD: About 2½ Cups **ACTIVE TIME:** 10 Minutes **TOTAL TIME:** 4 to 24 Hours

INGREDIENTS

2 cups apple cider

¼ cup olive oil

Juice of ½ lemon

2 sprigs fresh thyme, leaves removed and minced

2 sprigs fresh rosemary, leaves removed and minced

2 garlic cloves, minced

1 tablespoon black pepper

2 teaspoons kosher salt

1 In a medium bowl or roasting pan, combine all the ingredients to the marinade and let rest for 15 minutes.

2 Add the desired meat into the marinade. Transfer to the refrigerator and let marinate from 4 hours to overnight. If the marinade does not fully cover the meat, turn the meat halfway through the marinating process so that all areas of the meat receive equal amounts of the marinade.

RED WINE & DIJON MARINADE

YIELD: About 1 Cup **ACTIVE TIME:** 20 Minutes **TOTAL TIME:** 3½ Hours

INGREDIENTS

¾ cup dry red wine

¼ cup olive oil

2 garlic cloves, minced

1 tablespoon Dijon mustard

1 tablespoon black pepper

1 tablespoon kosher salt

1 teaspoon minced fresh rosemary,

1 Place all of the ingredients in a large bowl that will be able to hold the meat. Refrigerate for about 45 minutes, then reserve a portion of the marinade.

2 Add the meat to the marinade and let marinate for 2 hours in the refrigerator. If the meat isn't fully submerged in the marinade, rotate it a couple of times.

3 A half-hour before roasting, remove the meat from the marinade and place on the roasting rack so that the marinade seeps from the meat. Discard the used marinade.

4 While cooking, baste the rib roast with the reserved marinade about every half hour.

FIVE-SPICE MARINADE

YIELD: 1½ Cups **ACTIVE TIME:** 10 Minutes **TOTAL TIME:** 4 Hours

INGREDIENTS

¾ cup soy sauce

¼ cup rice vinegar

2 tablespoons peeled and minced fresh ginger

2 teaspoons sesame oil

2 teaspoons Chinese five-spice powder

¼ cup olive oil

1 teaspoon black pepper

1 In a bowl, combine all of the ingredients until they are thoroughly mixed.

2 Apply marinade to meat immediately and marinate for at least 4 hours.

CITRUS MARINADE

YIELD: About 2 Cups **ACTIVE TIME:** 15 Minutes **TOTAL TIME:** 2 Hours and 15 Minutes

INGREDIENTS

¾ cup orange juice

½ lime, juiced

½ lemon, juiced

¼ cup minced fresh cilantro

¼ cup olive oil

2 tablespoons minced fresh rosemary

4 garlic cloves, minced

1 tablespoon black pepper

1 tablespoon kosher salt

1 Put all of the ingredients in a bowl large enough to also accommodate the meat.

2 Add the meat to the marinade and let marinate for 2 hours in the refrigerator. The meat will not be fully submerged in the marinade, so be sure to rotate it throughout the marinating process in order for all sides of the meat to receive equal marinating time.

3 A half-hour before roasting, remove the meat from the marinade and place on the roasting rack so that the marinade seeps from the meat. Discard the remaining marinade.

BALSAMIC MARINADE

YIELD: About 2 Cups **ACTIVE TIME:** 10 Minutes **TOTAL TIME:** 4 to 24 Hours

INGREDIENTS

4 sprigs fresh basil

2 sprigs fresh rosemary, leaves removed

2 garlic cloves, crushed

2 teaspoons Dijon mustard

1 teaspoon raw honey

1 cup olive oil

¼ cup balsamic vinegar

1 tablespoon black pepper

1 tablespoon kosher salt

1 In a medium bowl or roasting pan, combine all of the ingredients and let rest for 15 minutes.

2 Add your desired meat into the marinade. Transfer to the refrigerator and marinate from 4 hours to overnight. The marinade may not fully cover the meat. In that case, turn the meat halfway through the marinating process so that all areas of the meat receive equal amounts of the marinade.

SWEET TERIYAKI MARINADE

YIELD: About 1 Cup **ACTIVE TIME:** 10 Minutes **TOTAL TIME:** 4 Hours

INGREDIENTS

½ cup soy sauce

¼ cup brown sugar

2 tablespoons rice vinegar

2 garlic cloves, minced

2 teaspoons peeled and minced fresh ginger

1 teaspoon black pepper

1 In a bowl, combine all of the ingredients until the sugar has dissolved completely.

2 Apply marinade to meat immediately and marinate in the refrigerator for at least 4 hours.

APPLE GLAZE

YIELD: 1 Cup **ACTIVE TIME:** 20 Minutes **TOTAL TIME:** 40 Minutes

INGREDIENTS

2 tablespoons olive oil

2 garlic cloves, minced

2 cups apple cider

1 teaspoon Dijon mustard

1 teaspoon minced fresh rosemary

1 teaspoon black pepper

2 teaspoons kosher salt

1 Heat the olive oil in a saucepan over medium heat. Add the garlic and cook until golden, about 2 minutes.

2 Add the apple cider, Dijon mustard, rosemary, black pepper, and sea salt to the saucepan. Cook until the sauce has reduced by half, about 6 to 8 minutes. Season to taste with additional pepper and salt.

3 Remove from heat, let rest for 10 minutes, and then apply to meat.

PINEAPPLE MARINADE

YIELD: 2 Cups **ACTIVE TIME:** 10 Minutes **TOTAL TIME:** 30 Minutes

INGREDIENTS

1½ cups pineapple juice

¼ cup brown sugar

¼ cup soy sauce

2 garlic cloves, minced

1 teaspoon kosher salt

1 In a bowl, combine all of the ingredients until the sugar has dissolved completely.

2 Place the meat in the marinade and marinate for at least 30 minutes.

BOURBON & SUGAR GLAZE

YIELD: About 1 Cup **ACTIVE TIME:** 10 Minutes **TOTAL TIME:** 40 Minutes

INGREDIENTS

4 tablespoons unsalted butter

½ cup bourbon

½ cup brown sugar

¼ cup apple cider vinegar

1 teaspoon Dijon mustard

1 teaspoon black pepper

1 teaspoon kosher salt

1 Place a saucepan over medium heat. Add the butter and cook until melted.

2 Add the bourbon, sugar, apple cider vinegar, and Dijon mustard to the saucepan. Add the pepper and salt. Bring to a simmer, cover the pan, and cook until the mixture has reduced by one-third, about 6 minutes.

3 Remove from heat and let settle to room temperature. Apply to meat before and during the cooking process.

STICKY BBQ GLAZE

YIELD: About 2 cups **ACTIVE TIME:** 5 Minutes **TOTAL TIME:** 5 Minutes

INGREDIENTS

1½ cups light brown sugar

3 tablespoons apple cider vinegar

3 tablespoons water

1 teaspoon red pepper flakes

1 teaspoon Dijon mustard

1 teaspoon black pepper

1 teaspoon kosher salt

1 Place all ingredients into a bowl and, using a fork, whisk until thoroughly combined. Apply to the meat before and during the cooking process.

KOREAN BBQ SAUCE

YIELD: 3 Cups **ACTIVE TIME:** 15 Minutes **TOTAL TIME:** 35 Minutes

INGREDIENTS

½ cup soy sauce

¼ cup ketchup

¼ cup rice vinegar

3 tablespoons light brown sugar

1 teaspoon gochujang

2 garlic cloves, minced

1 teaspoon sesame oil

1 teaspoon peeled and grated fresh ginger

4 scallions, chopped

1 teaspoon black pepper

1 Place a small saucepan over medium heat.

2 Add the soy sauce, ketchup, rice wine vinegar, light brown sugar, gochujang, and minced garlic into the saucepan, and stir until thoroughly combined. Bring to a simmer, cover the saucepan, and let simmer for 15 to 20 minutes, until the sauce has reduced by half.

3 Stir in the remaining ingredients, cook for 2 more minutes, and remove from heat.

4 Let the sauce stand for 10 minutes before serving.

MADEIRA SAUCE

YIELD: 1½ Cups **ACTIVE TIME:** 20 Minutes **TOTAL TIME:** 25 Minutes

INGREDIENTS

2 tablespoons unsalted butter

1 small shallot, minced

1 tablespoon all-purpose flour

¼ cup dry red wine

¾ cup Madeira

1 cup beef stock (for homemade, see page 274)

2 sprigs fresh thyme, leaves removed

2 sprigs fresh rosemary, leaves removed

Salt and pepper, to taste

1 Place the butter in a medium cast-iron skillet and warm over medium heat. Then add the shallot and sauté until translucent, about 4 minutes.

2 Add the flour to the pan and cook, stirring constantly, for 1 minute. Once incorporated, reduce heat to medium-low and then add the dry red wine, Madeira, stock, thyme, and rosemary.

3 Cook until the sauce reduced to your desired consistency, about 15 to 20 minutes.

4 When the sauce is reduced, remove the skillet from heat and season with salt and pepper. Spoon the Madeira sauce over the meat of choice.

TIP: If you want a stronger Madeira sauce, add 1 tablespoon of demi-glace to the sauce along with the beef stock. You can find demi-glace at the grocery store near the broths and stocks.

MAPLE BBQ SAUCE

YIELD: 1 Cup **ACTIVE TIME:** 10 Minutes **TOTAL TIME:** 25 Minutes

INGREDIENTS

¼ small white onion, minced

2 garlic cloves, minced

1 cup ketchup

3 tablespoons apple cider vinegar

1 tablespoon unsalted butter, clarified

½ cup maple syrup

2 tablespoons molasses

2 teaspoons mustard powder

Salt and pepper, to taste

1 Place a medium saucepan over medium-high heat. When hot, add the onion and garlic and cook until the onion is translucent and the garlic is golden, not brown—about 1 to 2 minutes.

2 Add the remaining ingredients and bring to a boil.

3 Reduce heat so that the sauce simmers and then cook, uncovered, for about 20 minutes.

4 When the sauce has reduced to about 1 cup, remove from heat and refrigerate for an hour before using.

SMOKED SOUTHERN BBQ SAUCE

YIELD: 2 Cups **ACTIVE TIME:** 35 Minutes **TOTAL TIME:** 55 Minutes

INGREDIENTS

2 to 3 cups hickory or oak woodchips

2 garlic cloves, minced

1 medium white onion, minced

1½ cups canned crushed tomatoes

½ cup tomato paste

¼ cup white wine vinegar

¼ cup balsamic vinegar

2 tablespoons Dijon mustard

1 medium lime, juiced

2 tablespoons peeled and minced fresh ginger

1 teaspoon smoked paprika

½ teaspoon ground cinnamon

2 dried chipotle peppers, minced

1 habanero pepper, seeded and minced (optional)

1 cup water

Black pepper, to taste

Sea salt, to taste

1 An hour before grilling, add the woodchips into a bowl of water and let soak.

2 Prepare a gas or charcoal grill to medium-high heat.

3 While waiting for the grill to heat up, place a small frying pan over medium heat and, when hot, add the garlic and onion and cook until the garlic has browned and the onion is translucent. Remove and set aside.

4 Transfer the cooked garlic and onion into a food processor, then add the tomatoes and tomato paste. Purée into a thick paste, and then add the remaining ingredients to the food processor and blend thoroughly. Transfer the sauce into a medium saucepan and set it near the grill.

5 When the grill is ready, about 400°F to 450°F with the coals lightly covered with ash, drain 1 cup of the woodchips and spread over the coals or pour in the smoker box. Place the medium saucepan on the grill and then bring the sauce to a boil with the grill's lid covered, aligning the air vent away from the woodchips so that their smoke rolls around the sauce before escaping. Let the sauce cook for about 30 to 45 minutes, every 20 minutes adding another cup of drained woodchips, until it has reduced to about 2 cups.

6 Remove the sauce from the heat and serve warm. The sauce can be kept refrigerated for up to 2 weeks.

SWEET MAPLE BBQ GLAZE

YIELD: 1 Cup **ACTIVE TIME:** 15 Minutes **TOTAL TIME:** 1 Hour

INGREDIENTS

1 tablespoon olive oil

2 garlic cloves, minced

¾ cup ketchup

1 cup apple cider

¼ cup maple syrup

2 tablespoons apple cider vinegar

1 teaspoon paprika

1 teaspoon Worcestershire sauce

1 teaspoon black pepper

1 teaspoon kosher salt

1 Heat the olive oil in a saucepan over medium heat. Add the garlic, and cook until browned, about 2 minutes.

2 Add the ketchup, apple cider, maple syrup, apple cider vinegar, paprika, and Worcestershire sauce to the saucepan. Bring to a simmer and cook for about 10 to 15 minutes, until the sauce has reduced by half. Season with pepper and salt.

3 Remove the glaze from saucepan and let cool to room temperature. Apply to the meat before and during the cooking process.

SNACKS

YOU'RE MAKING RIBS, but to do them right takes time. You and yours might need some food to nibble on as you wait, especially if you happen to be sipping whiskey to help pass the hours. These snacks will stave off the hunger before the main event.

CALIFORNIA GUACAMOLE

YIELD: 2 Cups **ACTIVE TIME:** 10 Minutes **TOTAL TIME:** 10 Minutes

Everyone should have a basic guacamole recipe on hand, as it is one of the finest things to do with an avocado. This recipe is a bona fide California classic.

INGREDIENTS

3 avocados, halved, seeded, and peeled

4 to 6 tablespoons lime juice, plus more for garnish

2 Roma tomatoes, seeded and chopped

1 red onion, chopped

1 to 2 garlic cloves, minced

½ teaspoon kosher salt

Black pepper, to taste

Old Bay seasoning, to taste

1 tablespoon minced fresh cilantro, for garnish

Tortilla chips, for serving

1 Place the avocados in a small bowl and mash roughly.

2 Add the lime juice, tomatoes, onions, garlic, salt, pepper, and Old Bay seasoning. Fold until everything is incorporated and the mixture has reached the desired consistency. While a chunkier guacamole is easier for dipping, pureeing the mixture in a food processor gives it a smoother finish.

3 Garnish with cilantro, top with a final splash of lime juice, and serve with tortilla chips.

BEET CHIPS

YIELD: 4 to 6 Servings **ACTIVE TIME:** 5 Minutes **TOTAL TIME:** 20 Minutes

You may have tried a commercial brand of beet chips from the supermarket, but they are quite easy to make at home. In this recipe, you don't even have to enlist a deep fryer to get crispy, addictive chips.

INGREDIENTS

5 beets, peeled and sliced very thin

¼ cup olive oil

2 teaspoons sea salt

1   Preheat the oven to 400°F. Place the beets and olive oil in a bowl and toss until the slices are evenly coated.

2   Place on a baking sheet in a single layer. Bake for 12 to 15 minutes, or until crispy.

3   Remove from the oven, transfer to a bowl, add the salt, and toss. Serve warm or store in an airtight container.

HOT & SPICY CARROTS

YIELD: 4 Servings **ACTIVE TIME:** 15 Minutes **TOTAL TIME:** 1 Hour and 30 Minutes

This is a quick pickle recipe that can be used with other vegetables. You can marinate them for up to 5 days, but they will have plenty of flavor in just an hour.

INGREDIENTS

1 lb. large carrots, peeled

1 cup unseasoned rice vinegar

1 teaspoon kosher or sea salt

2 tablespoons granulated sugar, plus 2 teaspoons

1 cup water

1 Wash the carrots and cut into matchsticks or rounds that are about the size of a quarter. Pat dry.

2 Place the vinegar, salt, sugar, and water in a bowl and stir until the sugar dissolves. Add the carrots to the mixture and marinate for at least 1 hour before serving.

3 For the best flavor, store vegetables in an airtight mason jar in the refrigerator for up to 5 days.

QUICK PICKLES

YIELDS: 2 Pints **ACTIVE TIME:** 15 Minutes **TOTAL TIME:** 12 Hours to 2 Days

This is a go-to recipe for pickles. It will produce classic cucumber pickles but also works well for carrots, green beans, or cauliflower.

INGREDIENTS

1 lb. fresh vegetables, such as cucumbers, carrots, green beans, summer squash, or cherry tomatoes

2 sprigs fresh herbs, such as thyme, dill, or rosemary (optional)

1 to 2 teaspoons whole spices, such as black peppercorns, coriander, or mustard seeds (optional)

1 teaspoon dried herbs or ground spices (optional)

2 garlic cloves, smashed or sliced (optional)

1 cup preferred vinegar

1 cup water

1 tablespoon kosher salt or 2 teaspoons pickling salt

1 tablespoon granulated sugar (optional)

1 Wash two wide-mouth pint jars, lids, and bands in warm soapy water and rinse well. Set aside to dry or dry by hand.

2 Wash and dry the vegetables. Peel the carrots, if using. Trim the ends of the green beans, if using. Cut the vegetables into desired shapes and sizes.

3 Divide whatever herbs, spices, and/or garlic you are using between the jars.

4 Pack the vegetables into the jars, making sure there is ½" of space remaining at the top. Pack them in as tightly as you can without damaging the vegetables.

5 Combine the vinegar, water, and salt in a small saucepan and cook over high heat. If using, add the sugar. Bring to a boil, while stirring to dissolve the salt and sugar. Pour the brine over the vegetables, filling each jar to within ½" of the top. You may end up not using all the brine.

6 Gently tap the jars against the counter a few times to remove all the air bubbles. Top off with more pickling brine if necessary.

7 Place the lids on the jars and screw on the bands until tight.

8 Let the jars cool to room temperature. Store the pickles in the refrigerator. The pickles will improve with flavor as they age, so try to wait at least 2 days before serving.

SPICY PICKLES

YIELD: 12 Cups **ACTIVE TIME:** 20 Minutes **TOTAL TIME:** 5 to 8 Hours

This is the perfect recipe to have on hand when cucumbers show up in the spring. With a little preparation, you can make sure you have enough of these delicious pickles to last all year.

INGREDIENTS

3 lbs. pickling cucumbers, sliced thin

3 small yellow onions, sliced thin

1 red bell pepper, stemmed, seeded, and sliced thin

2 habanero peppers, stemmed, seeded, and sliced thin

3 garlic cloves, sliced

3 cups granulated sugar

3 cups apple cider vinegar

2 tablespoons mustard seeds

2 teaspoons ground turmeric

1 teaspoon black pepper

⅓ cup canning and pickling salt

1 Place the cucumbers, onions, peppers, and garlic in a large bowl.

2 Place the sugar, apple cider vinegar, mustard seeds, turmeric, and pepper in a large pot and bring to a boil over medium-high heat, stirring to dissolve the sugar.

3 Add the vegetables and the salt and return to a boil. Remove the pot from heat and let it cool slightly.

4 Fill sterilized mason jars with the vegetables and cover with the brine. Place the lids on the jars and secure the bands tightly. Place the jars in the boiling water for 40 minutes.

5 Use the tongs to remove the jars from the boiling water and let them cool. As they are cooling, you should hear the classic "ping and pop" sound of the lids creating a seal.

6 After 4 to 6 hours, check the lids. There should be no give in them, and they should be suctioned onto the jars. Discard any lids and food that did not seal properly. Store the pickles in a cool, dark place for up to 1 year.

BLACK BEAN HUMMUS

YIELD: 4 Cups **ACTIVE TIME:** 10 Minutes **TOTAL TIME:** 10 Minutes

A new take on hummus that blends black beans with the usual suspects (tahini) plus a few unusual ones (anchovy paste). This flavorful dip works with crudité or warm pita bread.

INGREDIENTS

2 (14 oz.) cans black beans, plus more as needed

¼ cup tahini

¾ cup lime juice

¾ cup olive oil

2 teaspoons sea salt

1 tablespoon black pepper

1 teaspoon Tabasco™

1 teaspoon anchovy paste

Water, as needed

Fresh cilantro leaves, chopped, for garnish

Pita triangles, warmed, for serving

Crudités, for serving

1   Place all of the ingredients, except for those designated for garnish or for serving, in a food processor and blend until the desired consistency is achieved. If too thick, add a tablespoon of water. If too thin, add more black beans.

2   Place in the serving bowl, garnish with the cilantro, and serve with warm pita triangles and crudités.

DILLY BEANS

YIELD: 5 Pints **ACTIVE TIME:** 10 Minutes **TOTAL TIME:** 1 Week

This is a classic preparation for green beans—perfect when they come in all at once in mid-summer.

INGREDIENTS

3 lbs. green beans

2½ cups white vinegar

2½ cups water

¼ cup pickling salt

5 garlic cloves

5 teaspoons dill seeds (not dill weed)

5 teaspoons red pepper flakes

1　Prepare a boiling water bath and five pint jars. Place lids and bands in a small saucepan and simmer over low heat while you prepare the beans.

2　Wash and trim the beans so that they will fit in the jars. If the beans are particularly long, cut them in half. Place the vinegar, water, and salt in a medium saucepan and bring to a boil.

3　While the brine heats up, pack your beans into the jars, leaving ½" of space free at the top.

4　Place 1 clove of garlic, 1 teaspoon dill seeds, and 1 teaspoon red pepper flakes in each jar.

5　Slowly pour the hot brine over the beans, leaving ½" free at the top. After the jars are full, use a chopstick or butter knife to remove the air bubbles. Add more brine if necessary.

6　Place the jars in the boiling water for 40 minutes.

7　Use the tongs to remove the jars from the boiling water and let them cool. As they are cooling, you should hear the classic "ping and pop" sound of the lids creating a seal.

8　After 4 to 6 hours, check the lids. There should be no give in them, and they should be suctioned onto the jars. Discard any lids and food that did not seal properly. Let the beans sit for at least 1 week before serving. They will keep in a cool, dark place for up to 1 year.

SHARED DRINKS

You've been busy getting the big meal ready. The ribs are cooking, the sides are coming together, and dessert is in the oven. Don't get bogged down playing bartender. With punch at the ready, your guests won't even bother you with a drink order.

SEAHORSE

1 (750 ml) bottle of Old Bardstown Bottled In Bond bourbon

1 gallon orange juice

2 cups orangic lemon juice

1 capful of blood orange bitters

1 cup simple syrup

Thick slices of bourbon-soaked star fruit, for garnish

Luxardo maraschino cherries and syrup, for garnish

1 Combine the cocktail ingredients in a large punch bowl and refrigerate for at least 1 hour. Garnish each drink with a slice of the bourbon-soaked star fruit, Luxardo cherries, and a drizzle of Luxardo syrup.

SPICED PUNCH

6 lemons

1 cup granulated sugar

8 bags of chai tea

4 cups boiling water

1 cup Four Roses bourbon

1 (12 oz.) bottle of ginger beer

Lemon wheels, for garnish

Cinnamon sticks, for garnish

Whole cloves, for garnish

Star anise, for garnish

Allspice berries, for garnish

1 Peel the lemons and set the fruit aside. Place the lemon peels and the sugar in a bowl, mash to combine, and let stand for 1 hour. Juice the lemons and strain to remove all pulp.

2 Place the tea bags in the boiling water and steep for 5 minutes. Remove the tea bags and discard. Add the sugar-and-lemon peel mixture to the tea and stir until the sugar is dissolved. Strain and discard the solids. Add the bourbon and the lemon juice, stir to combine, and chill the punch in the refrigerator.

3 Add the ginger beer before serving and garnish each drink with lemon wheels and the spices.

HOT APPLE CIDER

8 cups apple cider

4 cups Four Roses bourbon

5 cinnamon sticks

3 orange peels, for garnish

30 to 40 whole cloves, for garnish

1 Place the apple cider, bourbon, and cinnamon sticks in a slow cooker and cook on low for 2 hours, making sure the mixture does not boil. Cut the orange peels into rectangles and press the cloves into them. Garnish each glass with a clove-studded orange peel.

MUSHROOM TOAST
WITH WHIPPED GOAT CHEESE

YIELDS: 4 Servings **ACTIVE TIME:** 10 Minutes **TOTAL TIME:** 45 Minutes

Toast is as basic as it gets, but you'd be surprised by how well it cleans up. The deep, nutty flavor of the chestnut mushrooms adds a new layer to this dish, but you can always substitute your favorite mushrooms if chestnut are unavailable.

INGREDIENTS

½ lb. chestnut mushrooms (or mushroom of your choice), sliced

2 tablespoons olive oil

Salt, to taste

4 thick slices sourdough bread

½ cup heavy cream

½ cup goat cheese

¼ cup sunflower seeds

2 tablespoons fresh rosemary leaves

1 tablespoon honey

1 Preheat the oven to 400°F.

2 Place the mushrooms on a baking sheet, drizzle with half of the oil, and sprinkle with salt. Place the mushrooms in the oven and roast until they begin to darken, about 10 to 15 minutes.

3 Place the slices of bread on another baking sheet, brush the tops with the remaining oil, and sprinkle with salt. Place the slices of bread in the oven and bake until toasted, about 10 minutes.

4 Place the cream in a mixing bowl and beat until stiff peaks begin to form. Add the goat cheese and beat until well combined.

5 Remove the mushrooms and bread from the oven and let cool for 5 minutes. Spread the cream-and-goat cheese mixture on the bread, top with the mushrooms, sunflower seeds, and rosemary, and drizzle with honey.

FRIED OKRA

YIELD: 4 Servings **ACTIVE TIME:** 10 minutes **TOTAL TIME:** 20 minutes

If you have reservations about trying a new food, there is a proven way to ease into it: fry it. Okra pairs very well with peppers of all kinds. Though the fried nuggets are good on their own, try adding a spicy jam or chutney for dipping.

INGREDIENTS

½ lb. okra, trimmed and cut into 2-inch pieces

Jane's Krazy Mixed-Up Salt, to taste

¼ cup cornmeal

¼ cup all-purpose flour

1 egg

Peanut oil, for frying

Salt, to taste

Spicy jam or chutney, for serving

1. Spread the okra on a baking sheet and sprinkle with the flavored salt.

2. Place the cornmeal and flour in a bowl and whisk to combine. In another bowl, beat the egg until scrambled.

3. Add the peanut oil to a Dutch oven until it is 2 to 3 inches deep. Warm to 350°F over high heat.

4. Dip the chunks of okra in the egg, transfer to the cornmeal mixture, and toss to coat.

5. When the oil is hot enough that a crumb of cornmeal sizzles, add all of the okra that will fit and fry. Keep an eye on them, turning gently as they brown. When brown on all sides (about 5 minutes), use a slotted spoon to remove them from the oil and place on a paper towel-lined plate. Let cool a few minutes and serve with the spicy jam or chutney.

PICKLED OKRA

YIELD: 2 Pints **ACTIVE TIME:** 15 Minutes **TOTAL TIME:** 5 to 7 Hours

Okra pickles beautifully, and looks incredibly appealing in an appetizer spread.

INGREDIENTS

1 lb. okra, trimmed

4 small dried red chile peppers

2 bay leaves

2 garlic cloves, halved

1 teaspoon dill seeds

1 teaspoon coriander seeds

1 teaspoon black peppercorns

1½ cups water

1½ cups apple cider vinegar

1½ tablespoons kosher salt

1   In a large saucepan, bring 6 cups of water to a boil. This will serve as your bath once the jars have been filled.

2   Pack the okra, chiles, bay leaves, and garlic cloves into 2 sterilized, 1-pint canning jars. Divide the dill seeds, coriander seeds, and peppercorns evenly between each jar.

3   In a medium saucepan, combine the water, vinegar, and salt and bring to a boil over high heat, stirring to dissolve the salt.

4   Pour the brine into the jars, leaving ½" of space free at the top. Apply the lids and bands.

5   Place the jars in the boiling water for 40 minutes.

6   Use tongs to remove the jars from the boiling water and let them cool. As they are cooling, you should hear the classic "ping and pop" sound of the lids creating a seal.

7   After 4 to 6 hours, check the lids. There should be no give in them, and they should be suctioned onto the jars. Discard any lids and food that did not seal properly. Store in a cool, dark place for up to 1 year.

ONION RINGS

YIELD: 4 Servings **ACTIVE TIME:** 15 Minutes **TOTAL TIME:** 20 Minutes

The secret to a great onion ring is not too much breading and using fine-grained salt, as kosher won't adhere to the onion.

INGREDIENTS

½ cup all-purpose flour

1 egg, beaten

⅓ cup whole milk

½ teaspoon paprika

½ cup plain bread crumbs

½ cup panko bread crumbs

1 tablespoon grated Parmesan cheese

Vegetable oil, for frying

2 large yellow onions, sliced into thick rings

Fine-grained salt, to taste

Creamy Adobo Dip (see recipe below), for serving

1 Place the flour in a shallow bowl, the beaten egg, milk, and paprika in another, and the bread crumbs and Parmesan in another.

2 Place a Dutch oven on the stove and add the vegetable oil until it is 2 to 3 inches deep. Heat the oil until a few bread crumbs sizzle immediately when dropped in.

3 Dip the onion rings in the flour, then in the egg mixture, and lastly in the bread crumb mixture. Make sure the rings are fully covered by the bread crumb mixture. Carefully drop into the hot oil and fry for several minutes until golden brown.

4 Using tongs, turn over to brown the other side (if necessary) and then transfer to a paper towel–lined plate.

5 Sprinkle with fine-grained salt, let cool briefly, and serve with the Creamy Adobo Dip.

CREAMY ADOBO DIP

INGREDIENTS

2 tablespoons mayonnaise

2 tablespoons sour cream

1 teaspoon adobo sauce (from a can of chipotles in adobo sauce)

1 Place all of the ingredients in a bowl, stir to combine, and serve.

REALLY RADISH
DIP

YIELDS: 2 Cups **ACTIVE TIME:** 10 Minutes **TOTAL TIME:** 10 Minutes

Though this is a simple dip to make using basic ingredients, the combination somehow tastes like a refined shrimp dip. While you might know it's a radish dip, go ahead and tell your guests it is shrimp dip, and see if the power of suggestion can turn a simple radish into a succulent shrimp.

INGREDIENTS

2 cups radishes

½ cup cream cheese, at room temperature

⅓ cup sour cream

2 tablespoons chopped fresh chives

Salt and pepper, to taste

Hot sauce, to taste

Crudités, for serving (optional)

Crackers, for serving (optional)

1 Roughly chop the radishes to the desired chunkiness of the dip and set aside.

2 Place the cream cheese and sour cream in a bowl and stir until smooth.

3 Fold in the chives and radishes and season with salt, pepper, and hot sauce.

4 Serve with crudités or crackers.

GRILLED GOAT CHEESE
APPETIZER

YIELDS: 4 Servings **ACTIVE TIME:** 5 Minutes **TOTAL TIME:** 15 Minutes

Without a doubt, the most famous chef in Argentina (and Uruguay) is Francis Mallmann. Renowned for his use of fire in cooking, he continually tries to return to and honor the most primal techniques while still elevating the ingredients. This recipe, which has been adapted to make indoors, remains a revelation. If you have the ability to make it over an open fire, try that as well. The additional smoke will be welcome.

INGREDIENTS

1 (8 oz.) log of goat cheese, sliced into 10 rounds

½ cup olive oil, plus 1 teaspoon

1 teaspoon red wine vinegar

1 cup dry, salt-cured black olives, pitted and chopped

¼ cup chopped walnuts

Large pinch of red pepper flakes, or to taste

2 teaspoons minced fresh oregano leaves

1 sourdough baguette, sliced and toasted

Salt and pepper, to taste

1   Arrange the goat cheese slices on a plate and place them in the freezer.

2   Place a cast-iron griddle or skillet over very high heat for 10 minutes.

3   Place the ½ cup of olive oil, red wine vinegar, olives, walnuts, red pepper flakes, and oregano in a bowl and stir to combine.

4   Lightly oil the griddle or skillet with the remaining olive oil. Place the cheese in a single layer and cook until brown and crusty on the bottom, about 2 minutes.

5   Use a spatula to remove the cheese and arrange the rounds on the toasted baguette slices. Spoon the olive mixture on top of the cheese, season with salt and pepper, and serve.

SUMMER VEGETABLE CHEESE DIP

YIELD: 4 to 6 Servings **ACTIVE TIME:** 20 Minutes **TOTAL TIME:** 1 Hour and 45 Minutes

This versatile dip is sure to be your go-to recipe. Its ability to accommodate leafy greens, slices of crusty bread, and almost any vegetable allows it to be used in any season.

INGREDIENTS

1 cup cream cheese or quark

½ cup sour cream

1 cup shredded mozzarella, plus more for topping

2 tablespoons fresh rosemary leaves

2 tablespoons fresh thyme leaves

½ cup diced summer squash

1 cup Swiss chard

1 cup spinach

6 garlic cloves, diced

2 teaspoons salt

1 teaspoon pepper

Slices of crusty bread, for serving

1 Place the cream cheese or quark, sour cream, and mozzarella in a bowl and stir until well combined.

2 Add the remaining ingredients for the dip, stir to combine, and place in the refrigerator for at least 1 hour.

3 Approximately 30 minutes before you are ready to serve the dip, preheat the oven to 350°F.

4 Transfer the dip to an oven-safe bowl, top with additional mozzarella, and bake until the cheese is melted and starting to brown, about 20 minutes. Remove from the oven and serve warm with slices of crusty bread.

TIP: Quark is a creamy, unripe cheese that is popular in Germany and eastern European countries. If you're intrigued, check out your local dairy farm.

PORK PÂTÉ
(AKA GORTON)

YIELD: 10 to 15 Servings **ACTIVE TIME:** 20 Minutes **TOTAL TIME:** 24 Hours

This French-Canadian delicacy is exceptional on slices of crusty bread, or used in a wrap or sandwich between meals, perfect for staving off peckishness at the grill.

INGREDIENTS

1 (3- to 5-lb.) bone-in pork shoulder

3 onions, sliced

2 teaspoons ground cloves

1 tablespoon salt, plus more to taste

4 dried bay leaves

2 teaspoons black pepper, plus more to taste

1 teaspoon nutmeg

1. Preheat the oven to 300°F. Place all of the ingredients in a Dutch oven and stir to combine. Cover, and cook over low heat until the pork falls apart at the touch of a fork, about 3 to 4 hours.

2. Remove from heat, discard the bay leaves, and transfer the pork shoulder to a plate. When the pork shoulder has cooled slightly, shred it with a fork.

3. Place the shredded pork and ½ cup of the juices from the pot in a blender. Puree until it forms a paste, adding more of the juices as needed.

4. Season with salt and pepper, transfer the paste to a large jar, and then pour the remaining juices over it. Cover the jar and store it in the refrigerator overnight before serving.

KALE CHIPS

YIELD: 4 Servings   **ACTIVE TIME:** 10 Minutes   **TOTAL TIME:** 30 Minutes

These chips are healthy, but no less satisfying because of it. This seasoning blend is simply a suggestion, so feel free to experiment with your favorite spices.

INGREDIENTS

1 bunch of kale, stems removed

1 teaspoon sea salt

½ teaspoon pepper

½ teaspoon paprika

½ teaspoon dried parsley

½ teaspoon dried basil

¼ teaspoon dried thyme

¼ teaspoon dried sage

2 tablespoons olive oil

1   Preheat the oven to 350°F.

2   Tear the kale leaves into smaller pieces and place them in a mixing bowl. Add the remaining ingredients and work the mixture with your hands until the kale pieces are evenly coated.

3   Divide the seasoned kale between 2 parchment-lined baking sheets so that it sits on each in an even layer. Place in the oven and bake until crispy, 6 to 8 minutes. Remove and let cool before serving.

OYSTER SLIDERS
WITH RED PEPPER MAYONNAISE

YIELD: 4 Servings **ACTIVE TIME:** 30 Minutes **TOTAL TIME:** 1 Hour and 15 Minutes

The briny taste of the oysters pairs well with the sweetness of the King's Hawaiian Rolls for a crunchy between-meals snack sure to satisfy.

INGREDIENTS

3 red bell peppers

1 cup canola oil

1 cup cornmeal

Salt, to taste

½ lb. oyster meat

2 eggs, beaten

1 tablespoon unsalted butter

4 King's Hawaiian Rolls

½ cup mayonnaise

1. Preheat the oven to 400°F.

2. Place the red peppers on a baking sheet and bake, while turning occasionally, for 35 to 40 minutes, until they are blistered all over. Remove from the oven and let cool. When cool enough to handle, remove the skins and seeds and set the flesh aside.

3. Place the oil in a Dutch oven and bring it to 350°F over medium-high heat.

4. Place the cornmeal and salt in a bowl and stir to combine.

5. When the oil is ready, dip the oyster meat into the beaten eggs and the cornmeal-and-salt mixture. Repeat until evenly coated.

6. Place the oysters in the Dutch oven and fry until golden brown, about 3 to 5 minutes. Remove from the oil and set on a paper towel-lined plate to drain.

7. Place the butter in a skillet and melt over medium heat. Place the buns in the skillet and toast until lightly browned. Remove and set aside.

8. Place the roasted peppers and mayonnaise in a blender and puree until smooth. Spread the red pepper mayonnaise on the buns, add the fried oysters, and serve.

ROASTED BEET SPREAD

YIELDS: 2 Cups **ACTIVE TIME:** 20 Minutes **TOTAL TIME:** 1 Hour and 30 Minutes

This earthy spread is best served with goat cheese and crusty bread.

INGREDIENTS

4 beets, peeled and cubed

¼ cup olive oil

½ teaspoon sea salt, plus more to taste

¾ teaspoon cumin seeds

¾ teaspoon coriander seeds

2 garlic cloves, minced, plus more to taste

2 teaspoons seeded and minced green chile pepper

2 teaspoons fresh lemon juice, plus more to taste

⅓ cup minced cilantro leaves

1 Preheat the oven to 400°F.

2 Line a baking sheet with parchment paper. Place the beets in a bowl with 2 tablespoons of the oil and ¼ teaspoon of the salt. Toss to coat.

3 Arrange the beets on the baking sheet in a single layer and roast for about 1 hour, tossing periodically, until the beets are tender. There should be about 2 cups of beets. Set the beets aside to cool.

4 Warm the cumin and coriander seeds in a dry skillet over medium-high heat for about 2 minutes, stirring constantly, until they release their fragrance and change color slightly. Be careful not to burn them or they will become bitter.

5 Grind the seeds in a spice grinder or crush with a mortar and pestle.

6 Place the beets in a food processor and add the remaining oil and salt, the ground seeds, garlic, chili, and lemon juice. Puree until well combined.

7 Taste and adjust the seasoning as needed. Transfer the dip to a bowl, stir in the cilantro, and serve.

EGGPLANT DIP

YIELDS: 4 Servings **ACTIVE TIME:** 20 Minutes **TOTAL TIME:** 1 Hour and 30 Minutes

This is a straightforward eggplant dip, much like baba ganoush but without the tahini. It is somewhat mild and is therefore a great opportunity to top with interesting spice blends. This recipe uses dukkah, an Egyptian seasoning made from coriander, cumin, sesame, and nuts; it will add a bit of crunch and plenty of flavor.

INGREDIENTS

1 large Italian eggplant, halved lengthwise

1 tablespoon olive oil, plus more as needed

1 onion, diced

2 garlic cloves, chopped

1 tablespoon maple syrup

Fresh lemon juice, to taste

Salt and pepper, to taste

2 tablespoons chopped tomato (optional)

1 tablespoon chopped fresh parsley or cilantro

1 tablespoon dukkah

Pita chips, for serving

1   Preheat oven to 350°F. Place the eggplant, cut-side down, on a greased baking sheet. Roast in the oven until the eggplant is very soft, about 30 minutes. Remove from the oven and let cool.

2   Place the oil and onion in a skillet and cook over medium heat until the onion is just beginning to brown, about 5 minutes. Add the garlic and cook 2 minutes more.

3   Remove the skin from the cooled eggplant and add the flesh to the pan. Cook the eggplant until it breaks down further and becomes extremely tender, about 5 minutes.

4   Remove from heat and add the maple syrup, lemon juice, salt, and pepper. For a smoother dip, puree the mixture. Otherwise, leave chunky. Let the mixture cool.

5   When cool, place it in a small bowl and top with the tomato, if desired and parsley or cilantro. Sprinkle the dukkah on top and serve with pita chips.

PICKLED TURNIPS

YIELDS: 2 Cups   **ACTIVE TIME:** 10 Minutes   **TOTAL TIME:** 24 Hours

Pickled turnips are popular in the Middle East to pep up grilled meats or stewed vegetables. This easy recipe is perfect for a mid-day snack while grilling.

INGREDIENTS

1 lb. Japanese turnips

4 cups rice wine vinegar

2 cups water

½ cup fish sauce

1¼ cups granulated sugar

¼ cup fresh lime juice

1   Remove the stem from the turnip and run the bulb under cold water until clean. Cut into even quarters and place in a container that can accommodate hot liquids.

2   Place the remaining ingredients in a medium saucepan and stir to combine. Bring the contents of the pot to a steady boil and then pour it over the turnips.

3   Cover the container with an airtight lid and let cool to room temperature. Once cooled, store in the refrigerator overnight before serving.

GREEN TOMATO CHUTNEY

YIELD: 4 to 6 Pints **ACTIVE TIME:** 35 Minutes **TOTAL TIME:** 5 to 7 Hours

This can be served with crackers or grilled flatbread, and is also very nice as a condiment for a grilled cheese sandwich with sharp cheddar.

INGREDIENTS

3 lbs. green tomatoes, chopped

1 large onion, chopped

2 tablespoons peeled and minced fresh ginger

2 garlic cloves, chopped

1 teaspoon mustard seeds

1 teaspoon ground cumin

1 teaspoon ground coriander

2 teaspoons kosher salt

½ cup honey or maple syrup

1 cup apple cider vinegar

1 cup raisins

1 Bring water to a boil in a large saucepan.

2 Place all of the ingredients in another large saucepan and bring to a boil. Reduce to a simmer and cook, stirring occasionally, until the onions and tomatoes are tender and the juices have reduced, 20 to 30 minutes.

3 Transfer the sauce to sterilized mason jars. Place the lids on the jars and secure the bands tightly. Place the jars in the boiling water for 40 minutes.

4 Use the tongs to remove the jars from the boiling water and let them cool. As they are cooling, you should hear the classic "ping and pop" sound of the lids creating a seal.

5 After 4 to 6 hours, check the lids. There should be no give in them, and they should be suctioned onto the jars. Discard any lids and food that did not seal properly. Store this chutney in a cool, dark place for up to 1 year.

POUTINE

YIELDS: 4 to 6 Servings **ACTIVE TIME:** 35 Minutes **TOTAL TIME:** 45 Minutes

A stone-cold Canadian classic that the recent celebration of comfort food has ushered into the mainstream. The squeak provided by the cheese curds is just one of the many pleasures available in this dish.

INGREDIENTS

4 cups vegetable oil

2 russet potatoes, cut into strips

Salt and pepper, to taste

4 tablespoons unsalted butter

¼ cup all-purpose flour

1 garlic clove, minced

4 cups beef stock (for homemade, see page 274)

2 tablespoons ketchup

1 tablespoon apple cider vinegar

½ tablespoon Worcestershire sauce

2 cups cheese curds

1   Place the vegetable oil in a large, cast-iron Dutch oven and heat to 275°F. Add the potatoes and fry for 5 minutes, while stirring occasionally. Use a slotted spoon to remove the potatoes, transfer to a paper towel-lined plate, and let them cool completely.

2   Heat the oil to 350°F. Add the cooled potatoes and fry until golden brown, about 5 minutes. Transfer to a paper towel-lined plate and season with salt.

3   Place the butter in a saucepan and warm over medium-high heat. When it is melted, add the flour and cook, while stirring, until the mixture is smooth, about 2 minutes.

4   Add the garlic and cook until soft, about 2 minutes. Stir in the stock, ketchup, vinegar, and Worcestershire sauce, season with salt and pepper, and bring to a boil. Cook, while stirring, until the gravy has thickened, about 6 minutes.

5   Remove from heat and pour gravy over each serving of fries. Top each with a handful of the cheese curds and serve immediately.

SIDES

SUCCULENT, FALLING-OFF-THE-BONE meat is what a meal of ribs is all about, but they taste all the better when accompanied with side dishes that complement the seasoning and also help cut across the charred goodness of pork, beef, or lamb. Like the ribs recipes here, these sides range from traditional to unexpected, but they're all delicious.

BLACK-EYED PEAS WITH COCONUT

YIELD: 4 Servings **ACTIVE TIME:** 10 Minutes **TOTAL TIME:** 9 Hours and 15 Minutes

Black-eyed peas have a wonderful starchiness and nutty taste that is utilized far too infrequently. You can use canned peas in this preparation, but fresh will be better.

INGREDIENTS

1 cup dried black-eyed peas, soaked in cold water for 8 hours

¼ cup coconut oil

1 yellow onion, peeled and sliced

2 tomatoes, chopped

1 habanero pepper, stemmed, seeded, and chopped

2 teaspoons Berbere Spice (see below)

1 cup coconut milk

1 cup chicken stock

1 cup fresh cilantro leaves, minced

1 Drain the black-eyed peas, place them in a Dutch oven, and cover with water. Bring the water to a simmer and cook until the black-eyed peas are tender, about 45 minutes. Drain and set them aside.

2 Place the coconut oil in the Dutch oven and warm over medium heat. When the oil starts to shimmer, add the onion, tomatoes, habanero, and Berbere Spice and sauté for 2 minutes.

3 Add the coconut milk and stock and bring to a simmer. Reduce the heat to low and gently simmer until the liquid has slightly reduced, about 10 minutes.

4 Return the black-eyed peas to the pot and continue to simmer for 15 minutes.

5 Stir in the cilantro and serve immediately.

TIP: This can be serve on its own or over quinoa, millet, or rice.

BERBERE SPICE

INGREDIENTS

1 teaspoon fenugreek

1 teaspoon red pepper flakes

2 tablespoons sweet paprika

½ teaspoon ground cardamom

1 teaspoon ground nutmeg

⅛ teaspoon garlic powder

⅛ teaspoon ground cloves

⅛ teaspoon cinnamon

⅛ teaspoon ground allspice

1 Use a mortar and pestle or spice grinder to combine all of the ingredients.

PUERTO RICAN RICE & PIGEON BEANS

YIELDS: 4 Servings **ACTIVE TIME:** 30 Minutes **TOTAL TIME:** 1 Hour and 10 Minutes

The crusty layer of rice that results when you make the rice in a caldera is known as *pegao*, and, like all delicacies, getting it right is an art. So don't be discouraged if you get it wrong the first time, and know that getting it is well worth doing it right.

INGREDIENTS

4 cups long-grain white rice

2 oz. uncured bacon

1 tablespoon garlic powder

1 tablespoon onion powder

1 tablespoon ground cumin

1 teaspoon dried oregano

1 tablespoon ground achiote
or turmeric

½ teaspoon black pepper

1 cup Sofrito (see below)

½ cup chopped yellow onion

1 tablespoon vegetable oil

2 tablespoons tomato paste

1 tablespoon capers

10 Spanish olives, chopped

1 (14 oz.) can of pigeon peas,
drained

5 cups water

2 teaspoons kosher salt

1 Place the rice in a colander and rinse it three times to remove excess starch. Set aside.

2 Place the bacon in a large, wide cast-iron caldera and cook it slowly over medium heat until it is very crispy, about 10 minutes. Transfer to a paper towel-lined plate. Leave the rendered fat in the pot. When the bacon is cool enough to handle, crumble it into bite-sized pieces.

3 Add the garlic powder, onion powder, cumin, oregano, achiote (or turmeric), and pepper to the pan and sauté for 20 seconds. Quickly add the Sofrito and onion, stir to combine, and cook for 3 minutes.

4 Add the rice and stir to combine. Cook for 3 minutes and then add the vegetable oil, tomato paste, capers, olives, and pigeon peas. Stir gently to combine and cook, without stirring, for 1 or 2 minutes to allow the bottom layer of rice to stick to the bottom of the pan. If you do not want the crispy layer of rice, skip this instruction.

5 Add the water and salt and bring to a boil. Turn off the heat and quickly drape a clean kitchen towel over the pot. Place the lid on top and wrap the cloth up around the lid, making sure it does not hang down or it will catch fire. Turn the heat to high. Cook for 30 seconds and then reduce the heat to low. Simmer for 35 minutes.

6 After 35 minutes, raise the heat to high and wait 1 minute. Turn off the heat and let it steam for 5 minutes. Fluff with a fork, garnish with the crumbled bacon, and serve.

SOFRITO

INGREDIENTS

1 red bell pepper, roasted, seeded,
and peeled

½ yellow onion, chopped

6 garlic cloves

¼ cup olive oil

Zest and juice of 1 lime

Leaves from 1 large bunch
fresh cilantro

1 teaspoon dried oregano

Large pinch of kosher salt

1 Place the ingredients in a blender and puree until smooth.

TIP: If you can find them, add a bunch of culantro and a cubanelle pepper to the blender for a more authentic Sofrito.

JALAPEÑO & CHEDDAR
CORNBREAD

YIELD: 12 Servings **ACTIVE TIME:** 15 Minutes **TOTAL TIME:** 55 Minutes

A simple batter with a burst of umami thanks to all that cheese. This will be somewhat spicy, so cut back on the jalapeños if you, or a loved one, prefer things mild.

INGREDIENTS

6 tablespoons unsalted butter

1 cup all-purpose flour

1 cup yellow cornmeal

½ cup granulated sugar

1¾ teaspoons baking powder

1½ teaspoons baking soda

1 teaspoon kosher salt

2 large eggs, beaten

2 cups buttermilk

3 green jalapeño peppers, stemmed, seeded, and minced

¼ cup grated cheddar cheese

¼ cup grated Monterey Jack cheese

1   Preheat the oven to 400°F.

2   Place the butter in a 10" cast-iron skillet and place the pan in the oven as it warms.

3   Place the flour, cornmeal, sugar, baking powder, baking soda, and kosher salt in a mixing bowl and stir to combine. Add the eggs and buttermilk and beat with a large spoon until you have a thick batter.

4   Add the jalapeño and the cheeses and stir to evenly distribute.

5   Remove the skillet from the oven and pour the melted butter into the batter. Stir to incorporate then pour the batter back into the skillet.

6   Place in the oven and bake until puffy and golden brown, about 40 minutes. Let cool slightly before serving.

TIP: This can also be made in a muffin tin.

CORNBREAD
WITH HONEY

YIELD: 16 Servings **ACTIVE TIME:** 40 Minutes **TOTAL TIME:** 2 Hours and 15 Minutes

---

Adding thick corn puree to a cornbread recipe adds a freshness straight cornmeal just can't approach.

INGREDIENTS

5 ears of corn

10 tablespoons unsalted butter

1 cup diced onion

1 tablespoon minced garlic

2½ tablespoons salt,
plus more to taste

2¾ cups heavy cream

2 cups all-purpose flour

2 cups cornmeal

¼ cup brown sugar

2 tablespoons baking powder

½ teaspoon cayenne pepper

½ teaspoon paprika

1½ cups honey

6 eggs

¼ cup sour cream

1 Preheat the oven to 400°F.

2 Place the ears of corn on a baking sheet, place it in the oven, and bake for 25 minutes, until the kernels have a slight give to them. Remove from the oven and let cool. When the ears of corn are cool enough to handle, remove the husks and silk and cut the kernels from the cob. Reserve the corn cobs for another preparation. Lower the oven temperature to 300°F.

3 Place 2 tablespoons of the butter in a large saucepan and melt over medium heat. Add the onion and garlic, season with salt, and cook until the onion is translucent. Set ¾ cup of the corn kernels aside and add the rest to the pan. Add 2 cups of the cream and cook until the corn is very tender, about 15 to 20 minutes.

4 Strain, reserve the cream, and transfer the solids to the blender. Puree until smooth, adding the cream as needed if the mixture is too thick. Season to taste and allow the puree to cool completely.

5 Place the flour, cornmeal, 2½ tablespoons of salt, sugar, baking powder, cayenne pepper, and paprika in a large mixing bowl and stir until combined. Place 2 cups of the corn puree, the honey, eggs, remaining cream, and sour cream in a separate large mixing bowl and stir until combined. Gradually add the dry mixture to the wet mixture and whisk to combine. When all of the dry mixture has been incorporated, add the reserved corn kernels and fold the mixture until they are evenly distributed.

6 Grease an 11 x 7" baking pan and pour the batter into it. Place the pan in the oven and bake until a toothpick inserted into the center comes out clean, about 35 minutes. Remove from the oven and briefly cool before cutting.

CLASSIC CORN BREAD

YIELD: 4 to 6 Servings **ACTIVE TIME:** 1 Hour **TOTAL TIME:** 3 to 4 Hours

If you're going to make bread in a cast-iron skillet, you have to make corn bread. In fact, many restaurants now serve corn bread right in a cast-iron pan.

INGREDIENTS

4 cups finely ground yellow cornmeal

¾ cup granulated sugar

1 tablespoon kosher salt

4 cups boiling water

1 cup all-purpose flour

1 tablespoon unsalted butter, melted, plus 1 teaspoon

2 eggs, lightly beaten

2 teaspoons baking powder

1 teaspoon baking soda

1 cup whole milk

1   In a large bowl, combine the cornmeal, sugar, salt, and boiling water. Stir to combine and let sit for several hours in a cool, dark place or overnight in the refrigerator. Stir occasionally while the batter is resting.

2   When ready to make, preheat oven to 450°F.

3   Add flour, the 1 tablespoon of melted butter, eggs, baking powder, baking soda, and milk to the batter. Stir to thoroughly combine.

4   Heat the skillet over medium-high heat and melt the teaspoon of butter in it. Add the batter.

5   Transfer the skillet to the oven and cook for 15 minutes.

6   Reduce the heat to 250°F and cook another 40 minutes, or until the bread is golden brown on top and set in the center.

CORN TORTILLAS

YIELD: 20 Tortillas **ACTIVE TIME:** 50 Minutes **TOTAL TIME:** 50 Minutes

You really should be making your own corn tortillas, as a warm tortilla lifted straight from a cast-iron griddle or skillet is a thing of beauty. The main ingredient, masa harina, is a corn flour that is available in most grocery stores.

INGREDIENTS

2 cups masa harina, plus more as needed

½ teaspoon kosher salt

1 cup warm water (110°F), plus more as needed

2 tablespoons vegetable oil or melted lard

1 Place the masa harina and salt in a bowl and stir to combine. Slowly add the warm water and oil (or lard) and stir until they are incorporated and a soft dough forms. The dough should be quite soft and not at all sticky. If it is too dry, add more water. If the dough is too wet, add more masa harina.

2 Wrap the dough in plastic (or place it in a resealable bag) and let it rest at room temperature for 30 minutes. It can be stored in the refrigerator for up to 24 hours; just be careful not to let it dry out.

3 Cut a 16" piece of plastic wrap and lay half of it across the bottom plate of a tortilla press.

4 Place a large, cast-iron griddle across two burners and warm over high heat.

5 Pinch off a small piece of the dough and roll it into a ball. Place in the center of the lined tortilla press, fold the plastic over the top of the dough, and press down the top plate to flatten the dough. Do not use too much force. If the tortilla is too thin, you will have a hard time getting it off of the plastic. Open the press and carefully peel off the disk of dough. Reset the plastic.

6 Place the disk on the hot, dry griddle and toast for 30 to 45 seconds. Flip over and cook for another minute. Remove from the griddle and set aside. Repeat the process with the remaining dough.

SKILLET MAC & CHEESE

YIELD: 6 to 8 Servings   **ACTIVE TIME:** 30 Minutes   **TOTAL TIME:** 1 Hour

There's nothing like homemade macaroni and cheese, but it can get messy when you have to use several pots and pans to make and serve it. Here comes your cast-iron skillet to the rescue!

INGREDIENTS

1 lb. elbow macaroni or preferred pasta

1 tablespoon kosher salt

3 tablespoons unsalted butter, at room temperature

3½ tablespoons all-purpose flour

1½ cups whole milk, at room temperature or slightly warmed

¼ cup sour cream

¾ lb. sharp white cheddar cheese, grated

¼ lb. Gruyère cheese, grated

Salt and pepper, to taste

Dash of cayenne pepper

1   Preheat the oven to 425°F.

2   Put the macaroni in a 12" cast-iron skillet and add cold water so that it reaches 1½ inches below the top. Stir in the salt, turn heat to high, and cook the macaroni for about 10 minutes. Test a piece after about 7 minutes. The pasta should be al dente—nearly cooked through but still a bit chewy. When it is cooked, drain it in a colander over a large mixing bowl so the water is retained.

3   Put your skillet back on the stove over medium heat and add the butter. When it's melted, stir in the flour, with a wooden spoon if possible, to prevent lumps from forming. Once it starts to bubble, start slowly add the milk, whisking constantly as you add it. Add about ½ cup at a time, being sure to whisk it in thoroughly before continuing. When all the milk is stirred in, let the sauce simmer over low heat until thickened, about 10 minutes.

4   Reduce the heat to medium-low and stir in the sour cream. When the mix is warm again, add the cheeses, stirring gently as they melt. Season with the salt, pepper, and cayenne.

5   Add the macaroni gently into the cheese sauce. If it seems too thick, add some of the reserved water. The consistency should be like a thick stew. When the noodles are hot, transfer the skillet to the oven.

6   Bake for about 15 minutes, then check. The dish should be bubbling and the cheese on top starting to brown. This takes somewhere between 15 and 25 minutes. Be careful not to let it burn. Let the macaroni cool slightly before serving.

MAC & CHEESE WITH BROWN BUTTER BREAD CRUMBS

YIELDS: 6 Servings **ACTIVE TIME:** 15 Minutes **TOTAL TIME:** 1 Hour

The cheese in this dish will stick to your ribs. Reserve it for those nights when you're especially hungry and can afford to relax after the meal.

INGREDIENTS

Salt and pepper, to taste

½ lb. elbow macaroni

7 tablespoons unsalted butter

2 cups bread crumbs (use panko for an extra crunchy top)

½ yellow onion, minced

3 tablespoons all-purpose flour

1 tablespoon yellow mustard

1 teaspoon turmeric

1 teaspoon granulated garlic

1 teaspoon white pepper

2 cups half-and-half or light cream

2 cups whole milk

1 lb. American cheese, sliced

10 oz. Boursin cheese

1 lb. extra sharp cheddar cheese, sliced

1 Preheat oven to 400°F.

2 Fill an enameled cast-iron Dutch oven with water and bring to a boil. Add some salt and then add the macaroni. Cook until slightly under al dente, about 6 to 7 minutes. Drain and set aside.

3 Place the pot over medium heat and add 3 tablespoons of the butter. Cook until the butter starts to give off a nutty smell and browns. Add the bread crumbs, stir, and cook until the bread crumbs start to look like wet sand, 4 to 5 minutes. Remove and set aside.

4 Wipe the Dutch oven out with a paper towel, place over medium-high heat, and add the onion and the remaining butter. Cook, while stirring, until the onion is translucent and soft, about 7 to 10 minutes. Add the flour and whisk until there are no lumps. Add the mustard, turmeric, granulated garlic, and white pepper and whisk until combined. Add the half-and-half or light cream and the milk and whisk until incorporated.

5 Reduce heat to medium and bring the mixture to a simmer. Once you start to see small bubbles forming around the outside of the mixture, add the cheeses one at a time, whisking to combine before adding the next one. When all the cheese has been added and the mixture is smooth, cook until the flour taste is gone, 10 to 15 minutes. Return the pasta to the pot, stir, and top with the bread crumbs.

6 Place in the oven and bake for 10 to 15 minutes. Remove the pot from the oven and serve.

TIP: If you can't find Boursin, whisk some cream cheese and a little softened butter together.

GRILLED CORN
WITH CHIPOTLE MAYONNAISE
& GOAT CHEESE

YIELD: 4 Servings **ACTIVE TIME:** 10 Minutes **TOTAL TIME:** 45 Minutes

The middle of summer, when the fresh corn hits the market, is the perfect time to make this dish. It's got it all—sweet corn, spice from the chipotle, and a soft, creamy landing thanks to the goat cheese.

INGREDIENTS

6 ears of corn

3 chipotle peppers in adobo

½ cup mayonnaise

¼ cup sour cream

1½ tablespoons brown sugar

1 tablespoon fresh lime juice

2 tablespoons chopped fresh cilantro, plus more for garnish

1 teaspoon kosher salt, plus more to taste

½ teaspoon black pepper, plus more to taste

3 tablespoons olive oil

½ cup crumbled goat cheese

6 lime wedges, for serving

1 Preheat the oven to 400°F.

2 Place the ears of corn on a baking sheet, place it in the oven, and bake for 25 minutes, until the kernels have a slight give to them. Remove from the oven and let cool. When the ears of corn are cool enough to handle, remove the husks and silk.

3 Preheat your gas or charcoal grill to 400°F. Place the chipotles, mayonnaise, sour cream, sugar, lime juice, cilantro, salt, and pepper in a food processor and puree until smooth. Set aside.

4 Drizzle the corn with olive oil, season with salt and pepper, and place on the grill. Cook, while turning, until they are charred all over.

5 Spread the mayonnaise on the corn, sprinkle the goat cheese on top, and garnish with additional cilantro. Serve with wedges of lime.

WATERMELON SALAD WITH RICOTTA & ARUGULA

YIELD: 4 Servings   **ACTIVE TIME:** 10 Minutes   **TOTAL TIME:** 15 Minutes

This light salad is the perfect way to keep a hot day from getting the better of you. Pitting the spicy bite of arugula against creamy ricotta and the refreshing sweetness of watermelon will keep you in the right state of mind to enjoy the savory goodness coming off the grill.

INGREDIENTS

4 cups arugula

2 tablespoons olive oil

Flesh of 1 large watermelon, cubed

1 cup ricotta cheese

Black pepper, to taste

1   Place the arugula in a salad bowl. Add the olive oil and toss to combine.

2   Divide the watermelon between four bowls and top each of them with a generous scoop of ricotta.

3   Add the dressed arugula, season with the black pepper, and serve.

MIDSUMMER
CORN & BEAN SALAD

YIELDS: 4 to 6 servings   **ACTIVE TIME:** 15 Minutes   **TOTAL TIME:** 24 hours

This is a great make-ahead recipe when the local corn is ripe. In fact, if it is really fresh with great flavor, you can skip the cooking part all together and use raw kernels. Dried beans bring the best flavor, but if you are pressed for time, use canned white or black beans. The maple syrup is meant to accentuate the sweetness of the corn, so add according to your personal preference.

INGREDIENTS

1 tablespoon olive oil

4 cups corn kernels (preferably fresh)

½ cup dried beans, soaked overnight

1 small Red Bell pepper, diced

1 small Green bell pepper, diced

½ red onion, diced

Juice of ½ lime

1 teaspoon cumin

Tabasco™, to taste

3 tablespoons chopped fresh cilantro

1 tablespoon maple syrup, plus more to taste

Salt and pepper, to taste

1   Place the oil in a wide sauté pan, add the corn, and cook over medium-high heat until slightly brown, about 5 minutes. Remove from heat and let cool.

2   Drain the beans and place in a saucepan. Cover with water. Bring to a boil, reduce heat to a simmer, and cook until the beans are tender, about 45 minutes. Drain and cool.

3   Place all of the ingredients in a salad bowl, toss to combine, and chill in the refrigerator for 2 hours.

4   Taste, adjust seasoning as needed, and serve.

SALAD WITH CHARRED LEMON DRESSING

YIELD: 4 to 6 Servings **ACTIVE TIME:** 20 Minutes **TOTAL TIME:** 30 Minutes

---

Charring the lemons adds an intriguing bit of smoke to this terrific twist on a simple vinaigrette.

INGREDIENTS

3 large lemons, quartered

1 cup olive oil

Salt and pepper, to taste

4 cups butter lettuce

6 radishes, sliced thin

2 tablespoons minced fresh chives

¼ cup grated Parmesan cheese

1 Place a large, cast-iron skillet over high heat for 5 minutes.

2 Add the lemons to the skillet and let them char.

3 Transfer the lemons to a large strainer set over a bowl. Use a large spoon to crush the lemons and let the juice fall into the bowl. Discard the lemon peels and seeds.

4 Stir in the olive oil, salt, and pepper. Taste and season accordingly.

5 Place the remaining ingredients in a salad bowl and toss to combine. Add half of the dressing, toss to coat, and serve with the remaining dressing on the side.

KIMCHI

YIELD: 4 Cups **ACTIVE TIME:** 30 Minutes **TOTAL TIME:** 3 to 7 Days

Simple and versatile, kimchi is the perfect introduction to all that fermentation has to offer.

INGREDIENTS

1 head napa cabbage, cut into strips

½ cup kosher salt

2 tablespoons peeled and minced fresh ginger

6 garlic cloves, minced

1 teaspoon granulated sugar

5 tablespoons red pepper flakes

3 bunches scallions, trimmed and sliced

Filtered water, as needed

1 Place the cabbage and salt in a large bowl and stir to combine. Work the mixture with your hands, squeezing to remove any liquid from the cabbage. Let the mixture rest for 2 hours.

2 Add the remaining ingredients, work the mixture until well combined, and squeeze to remove as much liquid as possible.

3 Transfer the mixture to a container and press down so it is tightly packed. The liquid should be covering the mixture. If it is not, add water until the mixture is covered.

4 Cover the jar and let the mixture sit at room temperature for 3 to 7 days, removing the lid daily to release the gases that have built up. When the taste is to your liking, store in an airtight container in the refrigerator.

ROASTED BRUSSELS SPROUTS WITH BACON, BLUE CHEESE & PICKLED RED ONION

YIELD: 4 to 6 Servings **ACTIVE TIME:** 15 Minutes **TOTAL TIME:** 50 Minutes

---

Brussels sprouts have a bad reputation with a lot of folks, but when seared and seasoned well, their savory, nutty flavor is a revelation, able to go toe-to-toe with rich ingredients like bacon and blue cheese.

INGREDIENTS

1 cup champagne vinegar

1 cup water

½ cup granulated sugar

2 teaspoons kosher salt, plus more to taste

1 small red onion, sliced

½ lb. bacon, cut into 1-inch pieces

1½ lbs. Brussels sprouts, trimmed and halved

Black pepper, to taste

4 oz. blue cheese, crumbled

1   Place the vinegar, water, sugar, and salt in a saucepan and bring to a boil. Place the onion in a bowl and pour the boiling liquid over the slices. Cover and allow to cool completely.

2   Place the bacon in a large sauté pan and cook, stirring occasionally, over medium heat until crisp, about 7 minutes. Transfer to a paper towel-lined plate and leave the rendered fat in the pan.

3   Place the Brussels sprouts in the pan, cut-side down, season with salt and pepper, and cook over medium heat until they are a deep golden brown, about 7 minutes.

4   Transfer the Brussels sprouts to a platter, top with the pickled onions, bacon, and blue cheese, and serve.

BASIC RED CABBAGE
SLAW

YIELD: 2 to 4 Servings   **ACTIVE TIME:** 10 Minutes   **TOTAL TIME:** 2 to 3 Hours

This is a topper that should be made a few hours ahead of time to give the cabbage time to soften.

INGREDIENTS

1 small red cabbage, cored and sliced as thin as possible

1 teaspoon kosher salt, plus more to taste

1 lime, juiced

1 bunch fresh cilantro, chopped

1   Place the cabbage in a large bowl, sprinkle the salt on top, and toss to distribute. Use your hands to work the salt into the cabbage, then let it sit for 2 to 3 hours.

2   Once it has rested, taste to gauge the saltiness: if too salty, rinse under cold water and let drain; if just right, add the lime juice and cilantro, stir to combine, and serve.

CARROT & JICAMA SLAW

YIELD: 2 to 4 Servings **ACTIVE TIME:** 5 Minutes **TOTAL TIME:** 5 Minutes

Carrots and jicama are both sweet, so they need a zesty dressing. Fresh lime juice will give them some zip and the cilantro adds a citrusy flavor. If you can find toasted pumpkin seed oil, it really gives this slaw some backbone. If not, olive oil also works. Don't go in thinking the ancho chile powder is spicy, as it adds just a hint of smoke.

INGREDIENTS

½ lb. carrots, trimmed and peeled

½ lb. jicama, peeled

1 to 2 tablespoons lime juice

1 tablespoons toasted pumpkin seed oil or olive oil

¼ teaspoon ancho chile powder

¼ cup minced fresh cilantro

Salt, to taste

1 Grate the carrots and jicama into a bowl and stir to combine.

2 Add the remaining ingredients and gently toss to combine. Taste, adjust the seasoning as needed, and serve.

SAUTÉED RED CABBAGE WITH APPLES, FENNEL & BALSAMIC

YIELDS: 4 Servings   **ACTIVE TIME:** 25 Minutes   **TOTAL TIME:** 30 Minutes

This is a lovely dish for fall when the weather cools.

INGREDIENTS

½ red cabbage, cored and sliced

3 tablespoons unsalted butter

¼ cup water

1 apple, peeled, cored, and diced

1 teaspoon fennel seeds

Salt and pepper, to taste

1 to 2 tablespoons balsamic vinegar

Brown rice or mashed potatoes, for serving

1   Place the cabbage in a large sauté pan with a tablespoon of the butter and the water. Bring to a boil and cover the pan. Let the cabbage steam until the thick ribs are tender, 5 to 8 minutes, then remove the lid and cook until the water has evaporated.

2   Add the remaining butter, the apple, fennel seeds, and pinch of both salt and pepper. Reduce heat to medium-low and cook, while stirring occasionally.

3   When the apples and cabbage have caramelized, add the balsamic vinegar, cook for another minute, and then serve with brown rice or mashed potatoes.

RICED CAULIFLOWER

YIELD: 2 Servings   **ACTIVE TIME:** 10 Minutes   **TOTAL TIME:** 10 Minutes

This simple dish provides the texture of rice with the nutritional benefits of cauliflower. It's hard not to enjoy, and is excellent on its own with a little butter, but if you know people on the keto diet, they'll be thrilled to see this as part of the spread.

INGREDIENTS

1 large head cauliflower, trimmed and chopped

¼ cup olive oil

Salt and pepper, to taste

1 Place the cauliflower a food processor and pulse until it becomes granular.

2 Place the oil in a large skillet and warm over medium heat. When the oil starts to shimmer, add the cauliflower, cover the pan, and cook until tender, 3 to 5 minutes.

3 Season with salt and pepper and serve.

HOME-STYLE BAKED BEANS

YIELDS: 6 to 8 Servings   **ACTIVE TIME:** 30 Minutes   **TOTAL TIME:** 1½ to 2 Hours

Images of cowboys and campfires will be dancing in your head thanks to this cast-iron skillet version of baked beans.

INGREDIENTS

6 strips thick-cut bacon

½ onion, diced

½ cup seeded and diced bell pepper

1 teaspoon kosher salt, plus more to taste

2 (14 oz.) cans pinto beans, rinsed and drained

1 cup barbecue sauce

1 teaspoon Dijon mustard

2 tablespoons dark brown sugar

Black pepper, to taste

1. Preheat the oven to 325°F.

2. Warm a 12" cast-iron skillet over medium heat and add half of the bacon pieces. Cook until its just starting to crisp up, about 6 minutes. Transfer to a paper towel-lined plate.

3. Place the remaining bacon in the skillet, raise heat to medium-high, and cook, turning the bacon often, until browned and crispy, about 10 minutes. Reduce heat to medium. Add the onion and bell pepper and cook, stirring occasionally, until the vegetables start to soften, about 6 minutes.

4. Add the salt, beans, barbecue sauce, mustard, and sugar. Stir, season with salt and pepper, and bring to a simmer.

5. Lay the partially cooked pieces of bacon on top and transfer the skillet to the oven. Bake for 1 hour, until the bacon on top is crispy and browned, and the sauce is thick. If the consistency seems too thin, cook for an additional 15 to 30 minutes, checking frequently so as not to overcook the beans.

6. Remove from the oven and allow to cool slightly before serving.

SOUTHERN COLLARD GREENS

YIELD: 4 to 6 Servings **ACTIVE TIME:** 30 Minutes **TOTAL TIME:** 2 Hours and 30 Minutes

---

Here's the thing about authentic Southern collard greens: when you think they are done, just keep cooking them.

INGREDIENTS

2 tablespoons olive oil

1 onion, diced

½ lb. smoked ham or bacon, diced

4 garlic cloves, diced

3 lbs. collard greens, stems removed, leaves chopped

2 cups vegetable broth

¼ cup apple cider vinegar

1 tablespoon brown sugar

1 teaspoon red pepper flakes

1 Place the oil in a large saucepan over and warm over medium-high heat. When the oil starts to shimmer, add the onion and sauté until translucent, about 3 minutes. Add the ham or bacon, reduce heat to medium, and cook until the ham or bacon starts to brown, about 5 minutes.

2 Add the remaining ingredients, stir to combine, and cover the pan. Braise the collard greens until they are very tender, about 2 hours. Check on the collards every so often and add water if all of the liquid has evaporated.

YU CHOY
WITH GARLIC & SOY

YIELD: 4 Servings **ACTIVE TIME:** 10 Minutes **TOTAL TIME:** 15 Minutes

Steaming yu choy keeps it tender and light. If the stalks are large, leave them to cook a little longer.

INGREDIENTS

1½ lbs. yu choy (if especially long, cut them in half)

¼ cup water

1 tablespoon olive oil

2 garlic cloves, chopped

½ tablespoon rice vinegar

1 tablespoon soy sauce

1 Place the yu choy in a sauté pan large enough to fit all of them, cover with the water, cover the pan, and cook over high heat.

2 After about 5 minutes, check the thickest stalk to see if it is tender. If not, cook until it is. Once tender, add the oil and the garlic. Sauté until the garlic is fully cooked but not browned, about 2 minutes.

3 Add the vinegar and soy sauce, toss to combine, and serve.

YU CHOY
WITH BLACK BEAN
GARLIC SAUCE

YIELD: 4 Servings **ACTIVE TIME:** 15 Minutes **TOTAL TIME:** 20 Minutes

Black bean garlic sauce is made from fermented black beans and soy sauce and you can find it in Asian markets or in the Asian section of most grocery stores. It is perfect with steamed yu choy because a spoonful makes for an intense, instant sauce. I like to add an extra clove of garlic to give it a fresh element.

INGREDIENTS

1½ lbs. yu choy, chopped into 3-inch pieces

¼ cup water

½ tablespoon olive oil

1 garlic clove, minced

1 tablespoon black bean garlic sauce

1   Place the yu choy in a sauté pan large enough to fit all the greens, cover with the water, cover the pan, and cook over high heat.

2   After about 5 minutes, remove the lid and cook until most of the water cooks off.

3   Add the oil and garlic and stir-fry until the garlic is fragrant, about 2 minutes.

4   Add the black bean garlic sauce, stir to coat, and cook until heated through. Serve immediately.

KOHLRABI SLAW
WITH MISO DRESSING

YIELDS: 4 Servings **ACTIVE TIME:** 10 Minutes **TOTAL TIME:** 10 Minutes

The Asian flavors of this coleslaw are just perfect beside barbecue ribs. If you have a mandoline, it will make quick work of slicing the vegetables. A hand grater will also work.

INGREDIENTS

For the Dressing

1 tablespoon white miso paste

1 tablespoon rice vinegar

1 teaspoon sesame oil

1 teaspoon peeled and minced fresh ginger

1 teaspoon soy sauce

3 tablespoons peanut oil

1 tablespoon sesame seeds

1 teaspoon maple syrup

For the Coleslaw

3 kohlrabies, peeled and julienned or grated

2 carrots, peeled and julienned or grated

¼ cup minced fresh cilantro

¼ cup shelled pistachios, crushed

1. To prepare the dressing, place all of the ingredients in a mixing bowl and stir to combine. Set aside.

2. To begin preparations for the coleslaw, place the kohlrabies, carrots, and cilantro in a separate bowl and stir to combine.

3. Drizzle a few spoonfuls of the dressing into the coleslaw and stir until evenly coated. Taste, add more dressing if desired, top with the pistachios, and serve.

CONFIT
NEW POTATOES

YIELD: 4 to 6 Servings **ACTIVE TIME:** 5 Minutes **TOTAL TIME:** 1 Hour and 10 Minutes

New potatoes are young potatoes that are pulled in early spring. They are sweeter than their mature counterparts, since the sugars haven't had time to develop into starches, and are so soft and tender that they don't need to be peeled.

INGREDIENTS

4 cups canola oil

5 lbs. new potatoes

Salt and pepper, to taste

1   Place the oil in a Dutch oven and bring it to 200°F over medium heat.

2   While the oil is warming, wash the potatoes and pat them dry. Carefully place the potatoes in the oil and cook until fork-tender, about 1 hour.

3   Drain the potatoes, season generously with salt and pepper, and stir to ensure that the potatoes are evenly coated. Serve immediately.

TIP: These potatoes should have plenty of flavor, but if you're looking to take them to another level, replace the canola oil with chicken or duck fat.

HERBED
POTATO SALAD

YIELDS: 4 to 6 Servings **ACTIVE TIME:** 10 Minutes **TOTAL TIME:** 25 Minutes

The two most common potato salads have either a mayonnaise dressing or a sweet vinegar dressing. The French have a different approach with shallots and herbs and a tangy vinaigrette that lets the natural sweetness of the potatoes come through. The dressing is poured on the potatoes when they are still warm, letting them soak up the flavor.

INGREDIENTS

1½ lbs. low-starch, new or red potatoes, cubed

½ cup olive oil

3 tablespoons white wine vinegar

2 tablespoons dry white wine

1 teaspoon whole-grain Dijon mustard

1 teaspoon kosher salt, plus more to taste

1 shallot, minced

Black pepper, to taste

2 tablespoons minced fresh parsley

2 tablespoons minced fresh chives

2 tablespoons minced fresh dill

---

1 Add the potatoes to a pot of water large enough to hold them all, bring to a boil, reduce heat, and simmer until tender, about 15 minutes.

2 While the potatoes are simmering, whisk together the oil, vinegar, wine, mustard, and teaspoon of salt.

3 When the potatoes are done, drain them and place them in a bowl. Add the vinaigrette and shallot immediately and gently toss, making sure to coat all of the potatoes. Let cool completely.

4 Taste and adjust seasoning as needed. Add the black pepper and fresh herbs, stir to incorporate, and serve.

MOM'S CREAMED SPINACH

YIELD: 4 Servings **ACTIVE TIME:** 20 Minutes **TOTAL TIME:** 25 Minutes

This version of a comfort food staple is made with cream cheese and lots of onion. Definitely use frozen spinach for this one, especially if you are feeding a crowd.

INGREDIENTS:

1 tablespoon unsalted butter

1 cup minced yellow onion

2 garlic cloves, minced

1 lb. frozen chopped spinach

½ lb. cream cheese, at room temperature

Pinch of ground nutmeg

1 teaspoon marjoram

Salt and pepper, to taste

1 Place the butter in a sauté pan and melt over medium heat. Add the onion and garlic and cook until the onion is just translucent, about 3 minutes.

2 Add the frozen spinach to the pan along with a few teaspoons water, cover the pan, and cook for a minute. Remove the lid, break the spinach up, and cook until it is completely thawed.

3 Add the cream cheese, nutmeg, and marjoram and stir to incorporate. Cook until the sauce has reduced and thickened, about 5 minutes. Season with salt and pepper and serve.

DESSERTS

IF YOU SPENT the entire day with the ribs, you've been at it for a while. Sure, your clothes might smell like smoke and you've been eating off and on for hours. But there's always room for a little something sweet, and perhaps a nightcap?

LEAF LARD PIECRUSTS

YIELD: 2 (9") Piecrusts   **ACTIVE TIME:** 12 Minutes   **TOTAL TIME:** 2 Hours

---

Leaf lard is the highest grade of lard, coming from the visceral fat around a pig's kidneys and loin. It is spreadable at room temperature, making it the perfect base for a flaky, flavorful piecrust. If you cannot locate it, substitute an equivalent amount of shortening.

INGREDIENTS

2½ cups all-purpose flour

1½ tablespoons granulated sugar

1 teaspoon kosher salt

6 oz. cold leaf lard, cubed

2 tablespoons unsalted butter, chilled and divided into tablespoons

5 tablespoons ice-cold water, plus more as needed

1 Place the flour, sugar, and salt in a bowl and stir until combined.

2 Add the lard and butter and use a pastry blender to work them into the flour mixture. Work the mixture until it is a coarse meal, making sure to smooth out any large chunks.

3 Add the water and continue to work the mixture until it is a smooth dough. If it feels too dry, add more water in 1-teaspoon increments. Form the dough into a large ball and then cut it in half. Wrap each piece in plastic wrap and place in the refrigerator for 2 hours before using. The dough will keep in the refrigerator for up to 3 days. It also freezes very well, and can be stored in a freezer for 3 to 6 months.

DOUBLE CHOCOLATE DECADENCE CAKE

YIELD: 8 to 10 Servings **ACTIVE TIME:** 10 Minutes **TOTAL TIME:** 1 Hour

The name of this recipe says it all: double the pleasure with this chocolate-frosted chocolate cake.

INGREDIENTS

For the Cake

6 eggs

1⅓ cups granulated sugar

1 stick unsalted butter, melted

½ cup sour cream

1 teaspoon orange zest

½ lb. chocolate, melted

1⅓ cups cake flour

⅔ cup all-purpose flour

1 cup cocoa powder

2 teaspoons baking powder

½ teaspoon baking soda

1 tablespoon kosher salt

Chocolate shavings, for topping

For the Frosting

10 tablespoons unsalted butter, at room temperature

1½ teaspoons pure vanilla extract

1¼ cups confectioners' sugar

4 oz. chocolate, melted and at room temperature

---

1 Preheat the oven to 350°F.

2 To begin preparations for the cake, place the eggs and sugar in the work bowl of a stand mixer fitted with the whisk attachment and beat on medium until pale and fluffy. Add the butter, sour cream, orange zest, and melted chocolate and beat until combined.

3 Sift the flours, cocoa powder, baking powder, baking soda, and salt into a bowl. Add the dry mixture to the batter and beat until just combined. Scrape the bowl as needed while mixing the batter.

4 Divide the batter between two greased round cake pans. Place them in the oven and bake for 20 to 25 minutes, until a toothpick inserted into the center of each comes out clean.

5 Remove from the oven and let cool for 10 minutes before removing the cakes from the pans and transferring to a wire rack to cool completely.

6 To prepare the frosting, use a stand or a handheld mixer to beat the butter until it is smooth. Add the remaining ingredients and beat until the mixture is light and fluffy, about 5 minutes, stopping to scrape down the bowl as needed.

7 When the cakes have cooled, spread some of the frosting on the top of one cake. Place the other cake on top and cover the entire cake with the remaining frosting. Sprinkle the chocolate shavings on top and serve.

PEACH COBBLER

YIELD: 4 to 6 Servings **ACTIVE TIME:** 30 Minutes **TOTAL TIME:** 1 Hour

A timeless classic, the tart sweetness of the peaches is the perfect compliment to rich vanilla ice cream.

INGREDIENTS

5 or 6 peaches, pitted and sliced

¼ cup granulated sugar

1 to 2 tablespoons all-purpose flour

1 (16 oz.) roll biscuit dough

1 teaspoon cinnamon

Whipped cream (for homemade, see page 247), for serving (optional)

Vanilla ice cream (for homemade, see page 256), for serving (optional)

1 Preheat the oven to 400°F and place a cast-iron skillet in the oven as it warms.

2 Place the peaches, sugar, and flour in a bowl and stir to combine. The amount of flour you use will depend on how juicy the peaches are; more juice means more flour. Remove the skillet from the oven, transfer the mixture into the skillet, and bake for 10 minutes.

3 Remove the skillet from the oven and arrange the biscuits on top of the filling, making sure the dough is evenly distributed. Sprinkle the cinnamon on top and return the skillet to the oven. Bake until the biscuits are golden brown and the filling is bubbling, about 12 minutes. Make sure not to burn the biscuit topping. Remove from the oven, let cool briefly, and serve with whipped cream or vanilla ice cream.

CHERRY PIE

YIELD: 4 to 6 Servings **ACTIVE TIME:** 30 Minutes **TOTAL TIME:** 1 Hour and 30 Minutes

---

Nothing beats the syrupy goodness of a freshly baked apple pie. Even the most voracious of rib eaters will find room for a slice of this dessert.

INGREDIENTS

4 cups pitted Rainier cherries

2 cups granulated sugar

2 tablespoons lemon juice

3 tablespoons cornstarch

1 tablespoon water

¼ teaspoon pure almond extract

2 Leaf Lard Piecrusts (see page 229)

1 egg, beaten

1 Preheat oven to 350°F. Place the cherries, sugar, and lemon juice in a saucepan and cook, stirring occasionally, over medium heat until the mixture is syrupy.

2 Combine the cornstarch and water in a small bowl and stir this mixture into the saucepan. Reduce heat to low and cook, while stirring, until the mixture is thick. Remove from heat, add the almond extract, and let cool.

3 When the cherry mixture has cooled, place the bottom crust in a greased 9" pie plate and pour the cherry mixture into the crust. Top with the other crust, make a few slits in the top, and brush the top crust with the beaten egg.

4 Place the pie in the oven and bake until the top crust is golden brown, about 45 minutes. Remove and let cool before serving.

LEMON SQUARES

YIELD: 12 to 16 Squares **ACTIVE TIME:** 15 Minutes **TOTAL TIME:** 1 Hour

The perfect mixture of citrus and sweet, these squares provide that hint of sugar you crave after a big meal, without weighing you down.

INGREDIENTS

1 stick unsalted butter

⅓ cup confectioners' sugar

1 cup all-purpose flour, plus 2 tablespoons

Pinch of kosher salt

2 large eggs, at room temperature

1 cup granulated sugar

⅓ cup lemon juice

1 tablespoon lemon zest

1   Preheat the oven to 350°F and grease a square cake pan with nonstick cooking spray.

2   Place the butter, ¼ cup of the confectioners' sugar, the 1 cup of flour, and the salt in a mixing bowl and work the mixture with a pastry blender until it is coarse crumbs. Press the mixture into the cake pan and bake for 20 minutes, or until it is set and lightly browned. Remove from the oven and set aside.

3   Place the eggs, granulated sugar, remaining flour, lemon juice, and lemon zest in a mixing bowl and beat with a handheld mixer on medium until well combined.

4   Pour the mixture over the crust and bake for 20 minutes, or until just browned. The custard should still be soft. Let the pan cool on a wire rack before dusting with the remaining confectioners' sugar and cutting into squares.

NIGHTCAPS

An after-dinner drink is always nice, especially after a day of cooking and entertaining that might have felt more like an event. Take a load off and indulge that sweet tooth with a bite of dessert, unless you prefer to sip your dessert.

NIGHTTRIPPER

1¾ oz. bourbon

¾ oz. Amaro

¼ oz. Strega

2 dashes of Peychaud's Bitters

1 strip of orange peel, for garnish

1   Place all of the cocktail ingredients in a mixing glass filled with ice and stir until chilled. Strain into a brandy snifter filled with ice and garnish with the strip of orange peel.

BOURBON BALL MILKSHAKE

4 scoops of vanilla ice cream (for homemade, see page 256)

2 oz. Buffalo Trace Bourbon Cream

2 oz. chocolate fudge

Chocolate syrup, to drizzle, plus more for garnish

Whipped cream, for garnish (for homemade, see page TK)

Candied pecans, for garnish (optional)

1   Place the ice cream, bourbon cream, and chocolate fudge in a blender and puree until smooth. Line the inside of a frozen glass with drizzles of chocolate syrup and pour the cocktail into the glass. Pour the milkshake into the glass and top with additional chocolate syrup, whipped cream, and, if desired, candied pecans.

THE ZEMURRAY

2 oz. bourbon

¼ oz. banana liqueur

¼ oz. Palo Cortado Sherry

2 dashes of Peychaud's Bitters

Dash of Angostura Bitters

1 Luxardo maraschino cherry, for garnish

1   Place all of the cocktail ingredients in a mixing glass filled with ice and stir until chilled. Strain into a chilled cocktail glass and garnish with the Luxardo maraschino cherry.

BOURBON COBBLER

1⅔ oz. Eagle Rare bourbon

⅔ oz. Luxardo

½ oz. simple syrup

3 strips of lemon peel

3 strips of orange peel

3 strips of grapefruit peel

1 lemon twist, for garnish

1   Place the cocktail ingredients in a mixing glass and stir until combined. Add a bit of ice, gently stir, strain into a wine goblet filled with ice, and garnish with the lemon twist.

STRAWBERRY RHUBARB PIE

YIELD: 6 to 8 Servings **ACTIVE TIME:** 20 Minutes **TOTAL TIME:** 1 Hour and 20 Minutes

Sweet strawberries, bitter rhubarb, and an irresistibly flaky crust make for the perfect ending to a large meal.

INGREDIENTS

2 pints fresh strawberries, hulled and halved

4 cups chopped rhubarb

1 cup granulated sugar

¼ cup cornstarch

Zest of ½ orange

Pinch of kosher salt

2 Leaf Lard Piecrusts (see page 229), chilled

All-purpose flour, for dusting

2 tablespoons unsalted butter

1 egg, beaten

1 Preheat the oven to 400°F and grease a 9" pie plate.

2 Place the strawberries, rhubarb, sugar, cornstarch, orange zest, and salt in a large mixing bowl and stir to combine. Set the mixture aside.

3 Place one of the crusts in the pie plate, fill it with the strawberry-and-rhubarb mixture, and dot the mixture with the butter.

4 Cut the other crust into 1-inch-thick strips. Lay some of the strips over the pie and trim them so that they fit. To make a lattice crust, lift every other strip and fold them back so you can place another strip across those strips that remain flat. Lay the folded strips back down over the cross-strip. Fold back the strips that you laid the cross-strip on top of, and repeat until the lattice covers the surface of the pie.

5 Brush the lattice crust with the egg, taking care not to get any egg on the filling. Place the pie on a baking sheet, place it in the oven, and bake for 20 minutes. Reduce the temperature to 350°F and bake until the filling is bubbling and the crust is golden brown, about 40 minutes. Remove and let cool before serving.

RICE PUDDING

YIELD: 6 to 8 Servings **ACTIVE TIME:** 30 Minutes **TOTAL TIME:** 30 to 35 Minutes

This creamy dessert is perfect for an end-of-the-season cookout, where everyone slowly drifts inside out of the first cold snap to enjoy a delicious, filling dessert.

INGREDIENTS

4½ cups whole milk

½ cup heavy cream

1 cup arborio rice

½ cup granulated sugar

3 strips orange zest

1 teaspoon cinnamon

½ teaspoon grated fresh nutmeg

1 teaspoon pure vanilla extract

½ teaspoon kosher salt

1 egg yolk

1 Combine milk, cream, rice, sugar, orange zest, cinnamon, nutmeg, vanilla, and salt in a medium saucepan and bring to a gentle boil. Reduce heat to low and cook for approximately 25 minutes, until rice is tender and mixture is thick. Stir while cooking to make sure rice doesn't stick to the bottom of the pan.

2 Remove the pan from heat and remove the orange zest. Let stand for 3 to 5 minutes. Add the egg yolk and whisk until thoroughly incorporated. Serve immediately or chill in the refrigerator for 5 minutes.

KEY LIME PIE

YIELD: 6 to 8 Servings **ACTIVE TIME:** 10 Minutes **TOTAL TIME:** 1 Hour

The Key lime tree is native to Malaysia, but the name of this golf ball-sized citrus comes from the Florida Keys, where the trees brought by the Spanish came to flourish—at least until the majority of the groves were wiped out by a hurricane.

When selecting Key limes, keep in mind that the green ones are actually unripe. They will have higher levels of acidity and tartness, which can be fine in some preparations, but for desserts you'll want to seek out yellow Key limes, as they are sweeter.

INGREDIENTS

2 cups heavy cream

¼ cup granulated sugar

⅓ cup fresh Key lime juice

1 tablespoon gelatin

½ cup sweetened condensed milk

1 Graham Cracker Crust (see page 247)

Whipped cream (for homemade, see page TK), for garnish

Key lime zest and/or Key lime wheels, for garnish

1 Place the cream in a mixing bowl and beat until soft peaks start to form. Add the sugar and beat until stiff peaks start to form.

2 Place the key lime juice and gelatin in a small saucepan and stir until the gelatin has dissolved. Cook over medium heat until the mixture starts to thicken, about 3 to 5 minutes. Remove the pan from heat and allow to cool slightly. Stir in the condensed milk and then fold this mixture into the whipped cream resulting from Step 1.

3 Pour the filling into the crust, cover with plastic wrap, and place in the refrigerator. Chill until set, about 45 minutes. Garnish with Whipped Cream and key lime zest and/or wheels.

GRAHAM CRACKER CRUST

YIELD: 9" Piecrust   **ACTIVE TIME:** 20 Minutes   **TOTAL TIME:** 50 Minutes

INGREDIENTS

1½ cups graham cracker crumbs

2 tablespoons granulated sugar

1 tablespoon maple syrup

6 tablespoons unsalted butter, melted

1   Preheat the oven to 375°F. In a large bowl, add the graham cracker crumbs and sugar and stir to combine. Add the maple syrup and 5 tablespoons of the melted butter and stir until thoroughly combined.

2   Liberally grease a 9" pie plate with the remaining butter. Pour the dough into the pie plate and lightly press into shape. Line with tin foil and fill with uncooked rice. Bake for 10 to 12 minutes until the crust is golden.

3   Remove from the oven, discard the rice, and allow the crust to cool before filling.

WHIPPED CREAM

YIELD: 2 Cups   **ACTIVE TIME:** 5 Minutes   **TOTAL TIME:** 5 Minutes

INGREDIENTS

2 cups heavy cream

1 teaspoon pure vanilla extract

1   Place the cream and vanilla in a bowl and whisk until soft peaks begin to form. Be sure not to over-mix, as this will result in butter.

2   Place in refrigerator until ready to serve.

CHOCOLATE CHEESECAKE

YIELD: 6 to 8 Servings **ACTIVE TIME:** 1 Hour **TOTAL TIME:** 24 Hours

The decadent richness of the chocolate pairs with the creaminess of the cheese stunning after-dinner treat.

INGREDIENTS

For the Crust
1 stick unsalted butter, melted

1 cup granulated sugar

1½ tablespoons water

⅓ cup unsweetened cocoa powder

1½ cups all-purpose flour

For the Filling
4½ cups cream cheese, at room temperature

1⅓ cups granulated sugar

4 eggs

2 tablespoons Blood Orange Curd (see below)

2 cups sour cream

For the Ganache
1⅓ cups bittersweet chocolate chips

3 tablespoons unsalted butter

1⅓ cups heavy cream

3 tablespoons granulated sugar

1. Preheat the oven to 350°F. To prepare the crust, place the butter and sugar in the mixing bowl of a stand mixer fitted with the paddle attachment. Beat at medium speed until the mixture is light and fluffy. Add the remaining ingredients and beat until fluffy.

2. Press the mixture into a 9" springform pan. Place the pan in the oven and bake for 30 minutes. Remove and let cool. Lower the oven temperature to 300°F.

3. To prepare the filling, wipe out the mixing bowl of the stand mixer. Add the cream cheese and 1 cup of the sugar and beat on medium speed until combined. Incorporate the eggs one at a time, scraping down the mixing bowl after each has been incorporated. Add the Blood Orange Curd, beat until incorporated, and pour the mixture into the crust. Place in the oven and bake until the center jiggles slightly, about 1 hour. Turn off the oven and leave the pan in the oven for 1 hour.

4. Remove the cheesecake from the oven and preheat the oven to 300°F. Place the sour cream and the remaining sugar in a mixing bowl and stir to combine. Spread this mixture over the top of the cheesecake. Place in the oven and bake for 20 minutes. Remove from the oven and let cool until just warm. Cover with plastic wrap and place in the refrigerator overnight.

5. Remove the cheesecake from the refrigerator and let come to room temperature as you prepare the ganache. To prepare the ganache, place the chocolate chips and butter in a mixing bowl and set aside. Place the cream and sugar in a saucepan and bring to a boil over medium heat, while stirring. When the sugar has dissolved, pour the mixture over the chocolate and butter and let stand for 5 minutes.

6. Stir the ganache until it is smooth and then spread it over the top of the cheesecake. Let the cheesecake stand for 10 minutes before serving.

BLOOD ORANGE CURD

INGREDIENTS
Yolks of 6 eggs

½ cup granulated sugar

Zest and juice of 2 blood oranges

Zest and juice of 1 lemon

1 stick unsalted butter, cut into small pieces and at room temperature

1. Place the egg yolks and sugar in a small saucepan and whisk to combine. Add the citrus zests and juices and cook, while stirring constantly, over medium-low heat, until the mixture is thick enough to coat the back of a spoon, about 10 minutes. Make sure that the mixture does not come to a boil as it cooks.

2. Strain through a fine sieve while gently pressing down with a rubber spatula. Add the butter, stir until melted, and refrigerate until chilled.

COCONUT DREAM PIE

YIELD: 8 Servings   **ACTIVE TIME:** 15 Minutes   **TOTAL TIME:** 1 Hour

The lightness of the cream paired with the tropical sweetness of the coconut will have you walking on air.

INGREDIENTS

1 (14 oz.) can of unsweetened coconut milk

1 cup whole milk

¾ cup unsweetened shredded coconut, lightly toasted, plus more for topping

10 tablespoons granulated sugar

3 eggs

4½ tablespoons cornstarch

3 tablespoons unsalted butter

2 teaspoons pure vanilla extract

2 teaspoons pure coconut extract

1 Leaf Lard Piecrust (see page 229), blind baked

Whipped cream (for homemade, see page 247)

1   Place the coconut milk, milk, shredded coconut, and ½ cup of the sugar in a large saucepan and stir to combine. Bring to a simmer over medium heat.

2   While the mixture in the saucepan is warming, place the eggs, the remaining sugar, and the cornstarch in a mixing bowl and whisk until the mixture is smooth.

3   While whisking constantly, incorporate the mixture in the saucepan into the egg mixture in ½-cup increments. When you have incorporated 2 cups of the warmed mixture, whisk the tempered eggs into the saucepan and cook, while stirring constantly, until the mixture is thick enough to coat the back of a wooden spoon. Remove from heat, add the butter, vanilla, and coconut extract, and stir to incorporate.

4   Fill the piecrust with the mixture, cover it with plastic wrap, and refrigerate until cool.

5   When the filling is cool, top with the Whipped Cream and the additional coconut and serve.

LEMONY RICE PUDDING PIE

YIELD: 6 to 8 Servings **ACTIVE TIME:** 10 Minutes **TOTAL TIME:** 2 Hours and 10 Minutes

The tartness of the lemon and the starchy-sweetness of the rice combine to stunning effect in this rich dessert perfect for a warm summer's day.

INGREDIENTS

3 cups Lemon Curd (see below)

2 cups whole milk

1 teaspoon pure vanilla extract

1½ to 2 cups cooked rice (brown rice preferred)

1 Graham Cracker Crust (see page 247)

1 cup whipped cream (for homemade, see page 247)

Cinnamon, for garnish (optional)

1 Place the Lemon Curd and milk in a large mixing bowl and whisk to combine. Add the vanilla and cooked rice and stir to combine.

2 Evenly distribute the filling in the piecrust, smoothing the top with a rubber spatula. Cover the pie with plastic wrap and place in the refrigerator for 2 hours.

3 Preheat the broiler on your oven. Remove the pie from the refrigerator and place it underneath the broiler. Broil until the top starts to brown, about 5 minutes. Remove and top each slice with whipped cream and cinnamon, if desired.

LEMON CURD

YIELD: 2 Cups **ACTIVE TIME:** 15 Minutes **TOTAL TIME:** 30 Minutes

INGREDIENTS

1 cup fresh lemon juice

4 teaspoons lemon zest

6 large eggs

1⅓ cups granulated sugar

2 sticks unsalted butter

1 Place all of the ingredients the mixing bowl of a stand mixer fitted with the paddle attachment. Beat on medium speed until well combined.

2 Pour the mixture into a saucepan and cook over low heat until it is thick enough to coat the back of a spoon, about 10 minutes.

3 Pour the lemon curd into a serving dish, place in the refrigerator, and chill until it thickens further.

RASPBERRY ICE CREAM CAKE

YIELD: 8 to 10 Servings **ACTIVE TIME:** 20 Minutes **TOTAL TIME:** 1 Hour and 20 Minutes

This cake is incredible when made with fresh raspberry preserves and homemade ice cream. The just-picked flavors of the black raspberries are hard to beat.

INGREDIENTS

1 large package of ladyfingers

1 pint vanilla ice cream (for homemade, see page 256)

1 (12 oz.) jar of raspberry preserves

1 pint black raspberry ice cream (for homemade, see page 256)

1 pint of fresh raspberries, for topping (optional)

Whipped cream (for homemade, see page 247), for topping (optional)

1 Line the bottom of a 9" springform pan with some of the ladyfingers.

2 Spread a layer of vanilla ice cream on top. Spread a thin layer of raspberry preserves on top of the vanilla ice cream and then add a layer of the black raspberry ice cream. Add another layer of raspberry preserves, top with ladyfingers, and repeat until you reach the top of the pan.

3 Place the pan in the freezer for at least 1 hour. When ready to serve, top each piece with fresh raspberries and a dollop of whipped cream, if desired.

VANILLA ICE CREAM

YIELD: 4 Cups **ACTIVE TIME:** 45 Minutes **TOTAL TIME:** 13 Hours

INGREDIENTS

3 cups heavy cream

1 cup whole milk

¾ cup granulated sugar

1 teaspoon kosher salt

Yolks of 5 large eggs, beaten

Seeds of 2 vanilla beans

1 In a medium saucepan, warm the cream, milk, sugar, and salt over medium heat. Stir until the sugar has dissolved.

2 While whisking constantly, add 1 cup of the warm milk mixture to the bowl containing the egg yolks. Add the tempered eggs to the saucepan and cook over medium heat until the mixture thickens enough to coat the back of a wooden spoon.

3 Add the vanilla seeds and remove the pan from heat. Strain into a bowl through a fine sieve and stir the mixture as it cools.

4 When the mixture has cooled completely, cover with plastic wrap and place it in refrigerator for 6 hours.

5 Remove the mixture from the refrigerator and pour it into an ice cream maker. Churn until the desired texture is achieved. Place the churned cream in the freezer for 6 hours before serving.

BLACK RASPBERRY ICE CREAM

YIELD: 4 Cups **ACTIVE TIME:** 30 Minutes **TOTAL TIME:** 24 Hours

INGREDIENTS

2½ cups heavy cream

1½ cups whole milk

1 cup granulated sugar

Salt, to taste

Yolks of 6 large eggs

1 teaspoon pure vanilla extract

5 cups fresh black raspberries

1 Place the cream, milk, sugar, and salt in a saucepan, warm over medium heat until it starts to bubble, and remove from heat. Take care not to let the mixture come to a boil.

2 Place the egg yolks in a glass mixing bowl and whisk to combine. While whisking constantly, add one-third of the warm milk mixture to the egg yolks. When incorporated, whisk the tempered egg yolks into the saucepan.

3 Cook over medium-low heat, while stirring constantly, until the mixture is thick enough to coat the back of a wooden spoon, about 5 minutes. Take care not to let the mixture come to a boil. Strain through a fine mesh sieve and stir in the vanilla. Set the mixture aside.

4 Place the raspberries in a blender and puree until smooth. Strain through a fine sieve to remove the seeds and then stir the puree into the custard. Cover and place in the refrigerator to chill overnight.

5 Pour the mixture in an ice cream maker and churn until the desired consistency is achieved. Place in the freezer for 6 hours before serving.

YOGURT CUSTARD PIE
WITH BLUEBERRY & BASIL JAM

YIELD: 6 to 8 Servings **ACTIVE TIME:** 45 Minutes **TOTAL TIME:** 3 Hours

Sweet and creamy, this light summer dessert is perfect for serving up while working the grill.

INGREDIENTS

For the Jam
2 pints fresh blueberries

¼ cup basil leaves, minced

⅔ teaspoon fresh lemon juice

⅔ cup granulated sugar

1 tablespoon water

For the Pie
1 cup plain Greek yogurt

2 eggs, lightly beaten

¼ cup granulated sugar

3 tablespoons fresh lemon juice

1 teaspoon pure vanilla extract

1 Graham Cracker Crust (see page 247)

1 cup fresh blueberries, for garnish

1   To prepare the jam, place all of the ingredients in a saucepan and bring to a boil over medium-high heat, while stirring frequently. Reduce the heat and simmer, while continuing to stir frequently, until the mixture has reduced by half and is starting to thicken. Remove from heat and let it thicken as it cools.

2   Preheat the oven to 350°F.

3   To prepare the pie, place the yogurt, eggs, sugar, lemon juice, and vanilla in a mixing bowl and stir to combine. Transfer the filling into the piecrust and use a rubber spatula to distribute it evenly and smooth the top.

4   Place the pie in the oven and bake until the filling is just set, about 25 minutes. A toothpick inserted at the edge of the pie will come out clean, but the center may look slightly undercooked. Remove from the oven and let the pie cool for 10 minutes.

5   Spread the cooled jam over the surface of the pie and arrange the blueberries on top. Place in the refrigerator and chill for 2 hours before serving. Place any leftover jam in a sterilized mason jar and store in the refrigerator for up to 1 week.

MIXED BERRY PIE

YIELD: 6 to 8 Servings **ACTIVE TIME:** 30 Minutes **TOTAL TIME:** 1 Hour and 30 Minutes

All the best tastes of summer are present in this delicious pie, which showcases the best berries the season has to offer.

INGREDIENTS

1½ cups fresh blueberries

1 cup fresh blackberries

1 cup fresh raspberries

1½ cups fresh strawberries, hulled and halved

1 tablespoon fresh lemon juice

½ cup light brown sugar

2 tablespoons cornstarch

½ cup unsweetened raspberry preserves

2 balls of Leaf Lard Piecrust Dough (see page 229)

All-purpose flour, for dusting

1 egg, beaten

1. Preheat the oven to 375°F and grease a 9" pie plate.

2. Place all of the berries and the lemon juice, brown sugar, and cornstarch in a large bowl and toss to combine. Transfer the fruit to a large saucepan and cook over medium heat until the berries start to break down, 7 to 10 minutes. Stir in the preserves, remove the pan from heat, and set the mixture aside.

3. Place the balls of dough on a flour-dusted work surface and roll them out to fit the prepared pie plate. Transfer one of the crusts to the pie plate and fill it with the berry mixture.

4. Cut the other crust into 1-inch thick strips. Lay some of the strips over the pie and trim the strips so that they fit. To make a lattice crust, lift every other strip and fold them back so you can place another strip across those strips that remain flat. Lay the folded strips back down over the cross-strip. Fold back the strips that you laid the cross-strip on top of, and repeat until the lattice covers the surface of the pie. Brush the strips with the beaten egg, taking care not to get any egg on the filling.

5. Place the pie in the oven and bake for 45 minutes, until the crust is golden brown and the filling is bubbling. Remove from the oven and let cool before serving.

BANANA CREAM TART

YIELD: 6 to 8 Servings **ACTIVE TIME:** 15 Minutes **TOTAL TIME:** 15 Minutes

Who can resist this classic pairing of chocolate and banana?

INGREDIENTS

2 cups pastry cream (for homemade, see page 265)

2 large bananas, sliced

1 Tart Pastry Shell (see page 265)

Whipped cream (for homemade, see page 247)

Chocolate shavings, for topping

1 Place the pastry cream in the bowl of a stand mixer fitted with the paddle attachment. Beat on low until it is smooth and creamy.

2 Stir the banana slices into the pastry cream. Pour this mixture into the tart shell and smooth the top with a rubber spatula.

3 Spread the whipped cream on top of the banana filling and sprinkle the chocolate shavings over the tart. Store in the refrigerator until ready to serve.

PASTRY CREAM

YIELD: 2½ Cups   **ACTIVE TIME:** 15 Minutes   **TOTAL TIME:** 1 Hour

INGREDIENTS

2 cups whole milk

1 tablespoon unsalted butter

½ cup granulated sugar

3 tablespoons cornstarch

2 large eggs

Pinch of kosher salt

½ teaspoon pure vanilla extract

1   Place the milk and butter in a saucepan and bring to a simmer over medium heat.

2   As the milk mixture is coming to a simmer, place the sugar and cornstarch in a small bowl and whisk to combine. Add the eggs and whisk until the mixture is smooth and creamy.

3   Pour half of the hot milk mixture into the egg mixture and stir until incorporated. Add the salt and vanilla extract, stir to incorporate, and pour the tempered egg mixture into the saucepan. Cook, while stirring constantly, until the mixture is very thick and boiling.

4   Remove from heat and pour the pastry cream into a bowl. Place plastic wrap directly on the surface to prevent a skin from forming. Place in the refrigerator until cool.

TART PASTRY SHELL

YIELD: 9" Pastry Shell   **ACTIVE TIME:** 30 Minutes   **TOTAL TIME:** 3 Hours and 15 Minutes

INGREDIENTS

Yolk from 1 large egg

1 tablespoon heavy cream

½ teaspoon pure vanilla extract

1¼ cups all-purpose flour, plus more for dusting

⅔ cup confectioners' sugar

¼ teaspoon kosher salt

1 stick unsalted butter, cut into 4 pieces

1   Place the egg yolk, cream, and vanilla in a small bowl, whisk to combine, and set aside. Place the flour, sugar, and salt in a food processor and pulse to combine. Add the pieces of butter and pulse until the mixture resembles a coarse meal. Set the food processor to puree and add the egg mixture as it is running. Puree until the dough just comes together, about 20 seconds. Transfer the dough onto sheet of plastic wrap, press into 6" disk, wrap, and refrigerate for at least 2 hours.

2   Approximately 1 hour before you are planning to start constructing your tart, remove the dough from the refrigerator. Lightly dust a large sheet of parchment paper or plastic wrap with flour and place the dough in the center. Roll out to 9" and line the tart pan with it. Place the pan containing the rolled-out dough in the freezer.

3   Preheat the oven to 375°F. Place the chilled tart shell on cookie sheet, line the inside of the tart shell with foil, and fill with uncooked rice. Bake for 30 minutes, rotating the shell halfway through.

4   After 30 minutes, remove the shell from the oven and discard the rice and foil. Leave the tart shell on the cookie sheet and place it on the upper rack of the oven. Bake until the shell is golden brown, about 5 minutes. Remove and fill as desired.

SALTED CARAMEL PECAN PIE

YIELD: 8 Servings **ACTIVE TIME:** 45 Minutes **TOTAL TIME:** 1 Hour and 30 Minutes

The salted caramel highlights the sweetness of the pecans for a mouth-watering twist on a classic pie.

INGREDIENTS

1 Leaf Lard Piecrust (see page 229)

½ cup chopped pecans

1½ cups mixed salted nuts

1¾ cups granulated sugar

⅓ cup dark corn syrup

¼ cup water

¾ cup heavy cream

2 tablespoons dark rum

1 teaspoon kosher salt

3 large eggs, beaten

1 Preheat the oven to 350°F and place the rolled-out piecrust in a greased 9" pie plate.

2 Place the pecans and the mixed nuts in a bowl and stir to combine. Set the mixture aside.

3 Place the sugar, corn syrup, and water in a saucepan and cook, while stirring constantly, until the sugar has dissolved. Raise heat to medium-high and continue to stir until the mixture comes to a boil and begins to turn dark brown, about 10 minutes. Remove from heat.

4 Stir in the cream, being careful as the mixture will spatter. Place the saucepan over medium-low heat, add the rum and salt, and cook, while stirring, until the mixture is smooth. Ladle into a large bowl and let cool.

5 When the mixture is cool, whisk in the eggs and pour the mixture into the piecrust. Sprinkle the nut mixture over the top, place in the oven, and bake until a knife inserted in the center comes out clean, about 45 minutes. Remove and let cool completely before serving.

CARROT CAKE

YIELD: 6 to 8 Servings **ACTIVE TIME:** 20 Minutes **TOTAL TIME:** 2 Hours and 15 Minutes

This classic dessert would be nothing without the richness of the cream cheese frosting. If you're worried about overindulging, you can always claim this dessert counts as a vegetable.

INGREDIENTS

For the Cake

2 cups shredded carrots, plus more for topping

2 cups granulated sugar

1½ cups all-purpose flour

1½ tablespoons baking soda

1 teaspoon kosher salt

1 tablespoon cinnamon

3 eggs

1¾ cups vegetable oil

2 teaspoons pure vanilla extract

½ cup walnuts, chopped (optional)

For the Frosting

½ lb. cream cheese, at room temperature

5 tablespoons unsalted butter, at room temperature

1 tablespoon sour cream

½ teaspoon pure vanilla extract

1¼ cups confectioners' sugar

---

1 Preheat the oven to 350°F.

2 To begin preparations for the cake, place the carrots and sugar in a mixing bowl, stir to combine, and let the mixture sit for 10 minutes.

3 Place the flour, baking soda, salt, and cinnamon in a mixing bowl and stir to combine. Place the eggs, vegetable oil, and vanilla extract in a separate mixing bowl and stir to combine. Add the wet mixture to the dry mixture and stir until the mixture is a smooth batter. Stir in the carrots and, if desired, the walnuts.

4 Transfer the batter to a greased round cake pan and place the cake in the oven. Bake until a knife inserted into the center comes out clean, about 40 to 50 minutes.

5 Remove the cake from the oven, transfer to a wire rack, and let cool for 1 hour.

6 To prepare the frosting, place the cream cheese, butter, sour cream, and vanilla in a food processor and blitz until smooth. Add the confectioners' sugar and blitz until it has been incorporated.

7 When the cake has cooled completely, apply the frosting to the top of the cake. Top each slice with additional shredded carrot before serving.

ORANGE & ROSEMARY SHORTBREAD

YIELD: 24 Cookies **ACTIVE TIME:** 20 Minutes **TOTAL TIME:** 2 Hours

The orange flavor pulls out the citrus notes from the rosemary, for a light shortbread that goes perfectly with a cup of tea (or bourbon, of course).

INGREDIENTS

4 sticks unsalted butter, at room temperature

¼ cup granulated sugar

¼ cup fresh orange juice

1 tablespoon orange zest

2 teaspoons finely chopped fresh rosemary

4½ cups all-purpose flour

Confectioners' sugar, to taste

1 Preheat the oven to 350°F and line two baking sheets with parchment paper.

2 Place all of the ingredients, except the flour and confectioners' sugar, in a mixing bowl and beat at low speed with a handheld mixer until the mixture is smooth and creamy.

3 Slowly add the flour and beat until a crumbly dough forms. Press the dough into a rectangle that is approximately ½" thick. Cover with plastic wrap and place the dough in the refrigerator for 1 hour.

4 Slice the dough into rounds and place them on the baking sheets. Sprinkle with confectioners' sugar, place in the oven, and bake until the edges start to brown, about 15 minutes. Remove and let cool before serving.

BEEF STOCK

YIELD: 6 Quarts **ACTIVE TIME:** 30 Minutes **TOTAL TIME:** 5 Hours and 20 Minutes

---

INGREDIENTS

10 lbs. beef bones

½ cup vegetable oil

1 leek, trimmed, rinsed well, and cut into 1-inch pieces

1 large yellow onion, unpeeled, cleaned root, cut into 1-inch pieces

2 large carrots, peeled and cut into 1-inch pieces

1 celery stalk with leaves, cut into 1-inch pieces

10 quarts water

1 teaspoon kosher salt

8 sprigs fresh parsley

5 sprigs fresh thyme

2 fresh bay leaves

1 teaspoon peppercorns

½ lb. tomato paste

1 Preheat oven to 350°F. Lay the bones on a flat baking tray, place in oven, and cook for 30 to 45 minutes, until they are golden brown. Remove and set aside.

2 Meanwhile, in a large stockpot, add the vegetable oil and warm over low heat. Add the vegetables and cook until the moisture has evaporated. This allows the flavor of the vegetables to become concentrated.

3 Add the water, salt, bones, aromatics, and tomato paste to the stockpot, raise heat to high, and bring to a boil.

4 Reduce heat so that the stock simmers and cook for a minimum of 2 hours. Skim fat and impurities from the top as the stock cooks. As for when to stop cooking the stock, let the flavor be your guide.

5 When the stock is finished cooking, strain through a fine strainer or cheesecloth. Place stock in refrigerator to chill. Once cool, skim the fat layer from the top and discard. This will produce about 6 quarts and will keep in the freezer for about 6 months.

METRIC CONVERSION CHART

U.S. Measurement	Approx. Metric Liquid Measurement	Approx. Metric Dry Measurement
1 teaspoon	5 mL	
1 tablespoon or ½ oz.	15 mL	14 g
1 ounce or ⅛ cup	30 mL	29 g
¼ cup or 2 oz.	60 mL	57 g
⅓ cup	80 mL	
½ cup or 4 oz.	120 mL	¼ lb. or 113 g
⅔ cup	160 mL	
¾ cup or 6 oz.	180 mL	
1 cup or 8 ounces or ½ pint	240 mL	½ lb. or 227 g
1½ cups or 12 oz.	350 mL	
2 cups or 1 pint or 16 oz.	475 mL	1 lb. or 454 g
3 cups or 1½ pints	700 mL	
4 cups or 2 pints or 1 quart	950 mL	

BOURBON APPENDIX

IF YOU KNOW more about ribs than bourbon, the following pages are a crash course in American whiskey, the nation's spirit.

WHISKEY, BOURBON & RYE: WHAT'S THE DIFFERENCE?

Here's how it works: bourbon, rye, Tennessee whiskey, and some moonshine are whiskey. But not necessarily the reverse. "Whiskey" is the term used to describe an aged spirit (of any determining length) that is distilled from grain.

All bourbon, rye, and Tennessee whiskey come from grain—primarily corn, rye, malted barley, and wheat.

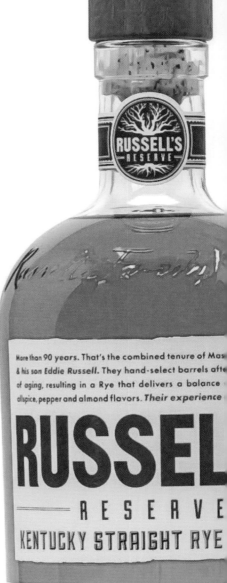

GRAINS

There are four main grains we are concerned with for this particular industry: corn, malted barley, rye, and wheat. These four grains, in some combination or another, make up the greater part of bourbon, rye, or Tennessee whiskey. They are the backbone of the industry.

Corn

Corn is the foundation of both Kentucky bourbon and Tennessee whiskey. It is the cornerstone of the industry in these two states. White, sweet corn is the coin of the realm, and the cornfields of the South and Midwest feed a steady stream of corn to distilleries throughout these two states.

Why corn? Because it helps offer that hint of sweetness which makes bourbon so popular here in the United States. Corn is where it all began!

Rye

The backbone of 90% of the bourbon and Tennessee whiskey market comes from rye. Rye offers the spicy notes that one associates with bourbon and whiskey. It lends a gingersnap-like quality, blending lots of spices with a peppery finish. The more rye in the mash bill, the drier and spicier the whiskey will be. Rye is one of the hardiest and easiest crops to farm, which is what made it the most popular grain grown for distillation before Prohibition.

Malted Barley

Malted barley is almost always in the mix. Malted barley provides several different elements. Firstly, it adds another texture or flavor profile to the whiskey. Because it is malted, which means it has been wetted and started to germinate, it provides enzymes that will help break down the grains, and help the yeast turn sugars and carbohydrates into alcohol.

Wheat

Most distillers use a red winter wheat in their mash. Wheat often lends a softer touch to whiskey, giving a soft, even sweet flavor not unlike that which oatmeal lends to a beer. Any whiskey with 51% or more wheat in its mash is a wheat whiskey, and bourbons that replace rye in the mash bill with wheat are "wheated" bourbons. Both lack the characteristic bite that comes from rye, and may have floral or grassy notes.

ALL WHISKEY IS NOT ALIKE

Here is a rundown on what differentiates the types of whiskey from one another.

CORN WHISKEY (also known as moonshine or white whiskey) is the base spirit most Kentucky and Tennessee whiskeys are made from. It is the distillate with water added back (usually), which comes from grain and some variable amount of corn. Some are made from 100% corn. It is usually clear. Most are not aged, but a few are "rested" in oak for a short period so that they can be called whiskey. Some moonshine contains cane sugar as part of the mash bill.

BOURBON is a whiskey made from at least 51% (but no more than 80%) corn, with the rest made up of rye, wheat and/or malted barley. It must be made in the United States, and aged in new charred oak barrels. The final product must be at least 80 proof. Although there is no minimum aging requirement for bourbon, any bourbon younger than four years must have an age statement on the label. Furthermore, the age statement of any bourbon must be according to the youngest whiskey in the bottle.

STRAIGHT BOURBON is American bourbon aged a minimum of two years, as mandated by law. This same requirement applies to any other whiskey labeled "straight." Moreover, any "bottled in bond" bourbon must also be a straight bourbon, and aged for at least four years (not to mention that it must come from a single distilling season, and be distilled by one distiller at one distillery, then aged at a federally bonded warehouse). Blended bourbon must contain at least 51% straight bourbon, but may also include other spirits, flavoring, and color.

RYE WHISKEY, like bourbon, is an American invention and must also be aged in new charred oak and bottled at at least 80 proof. Made from at least 51% rye grain, rye whiskey is spicier and drier than other varieties. Once common throughout the northeastern United States, rye whiskey almost died out after Prohibition, but is currently seeing a resurgence. Canadian whisky is also often called rye whisky, but most contemporary Canadian whiskies don't contain a majority of rye in their mash bill, or any at all.

TENNESSEE WHISKEY is made using the same method and ingredients as most bourbons, but features an extra step, a charcoal "mellowing" known as the Lincoln County Process, where the distillate is passed through a container (however big or small) of heavily charred American maple chips before it is put into new American oak barrels for aging. Although there are no legal guidelines as to how much charcoal the distillate must pass through to qualify as Tennessee whiskey, Jack Daniels and George Dickel filter their whiskeys through massive 10- and 13-foot vats of charcoal, respectively.

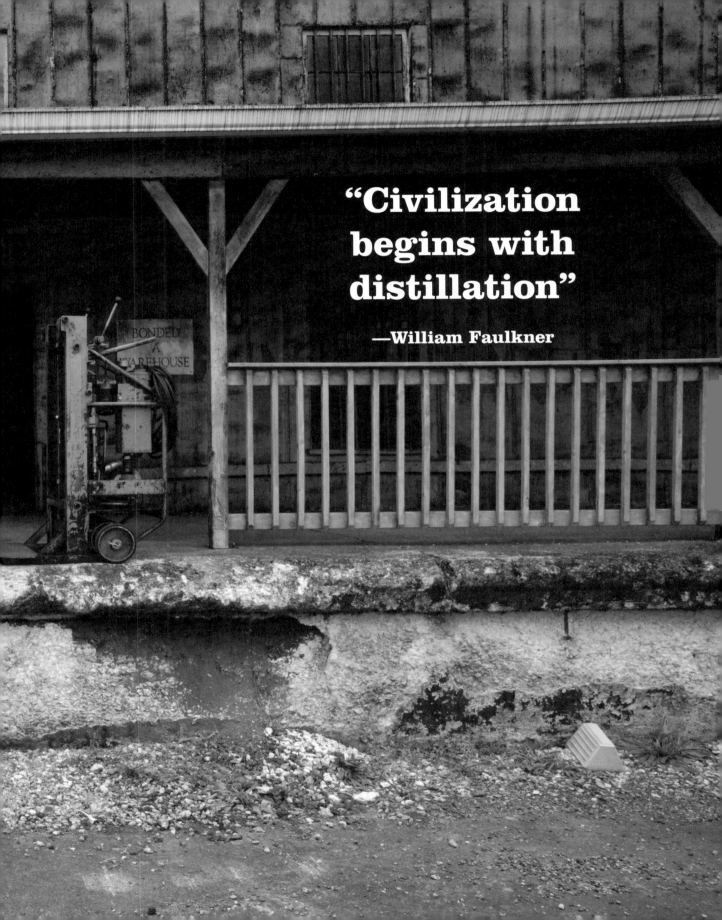

NORTHEAST REGION DISTILLERIES

Maine
Liquid Riot Bottling Co.
Wiggly Bridge Distillery

New York
Black Button Distilling
Black Dirt Distillery
Breuckelen Distilling
Kings County Distillery
Taconic Distillery
Tuthilltown Spirits
Widow Jane Distillery

Pennsylvania
Bluebird Distilling
Manatawny Still Works
Mountain Laurel Spirits
New Liberty Distillery
Stoll & Wolfe Distillery
Wigle Whiskey

Rhode Island
Sons of Liberty Beer & Spirits Co.

Vermont:
Appalachian Gap Distillery
WhistlePig Farm

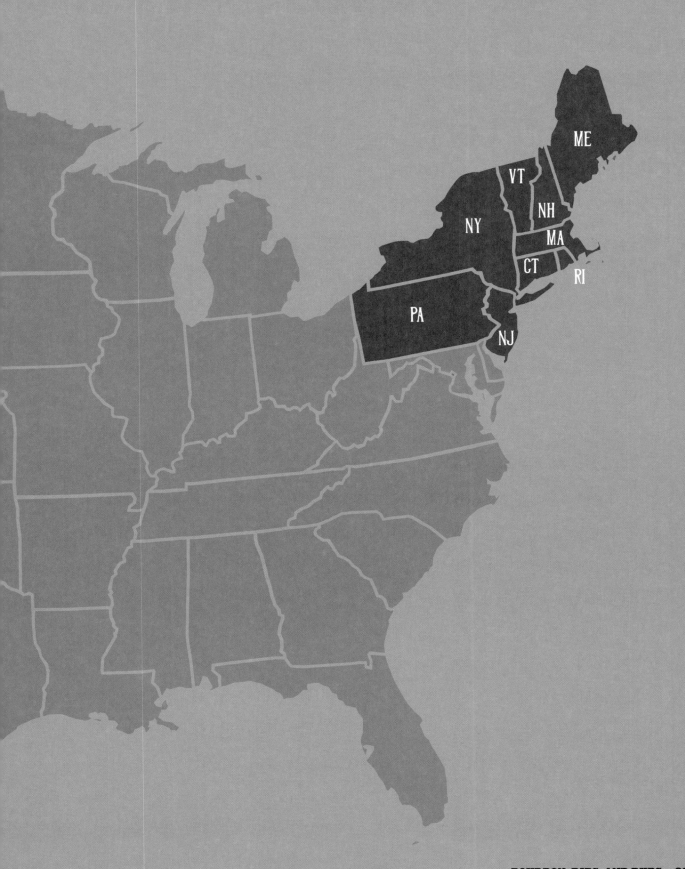

SOUTHEAST REGION DISTILLERIES

Alabama
Conecuh Ridge Distillery

Delaware
Painted Stave Distilling

Georgia
Lovell Brothers Whiskey

Kentucky
Angel's Envy Distillery
Barrell Craft Spirits
Barrel House Distilling Co.
Beam Suntory (Jim Beam Distillery, Booker Noe Distillery, and Maker's Mark Distillery)
Boone County Distilling
Brown-Forman Corporation
Woodford Reserve Diageo
Four Roses Distillery
Hartfield & Co.
Heaven Hill Distillery (Bernheim Facility)
James E. Pepper Distillery
Kentucky Peerless Distilling Co.
Limestone Branch Distillery
Lux Row Distillers
MB Roland Distillery
Michter's Distillery
New Riff Distilling
Old Pogue Distillery
Rabbit Hole Distillery

Sazerac (Includes Barton 1792 Distillery and Buffalo Trace Distillery)
Town Branch Distillery
Wilderness Trail Distillery
Wild Turkey Distillery
Willett Distillery

Maryland
Baltimore Spirits Co.
Sagamore Spirit

North Carolina
Blue Ridge Distilling Co.
Southern Grace Distilleries

Tennessee
Cascade Hollow Distilling Company
Chattanooga Whiskey Company
Corsair Distillery
Jack Daniel's Distillery (Brown-Forman Corporation)
Nelson's Green Brier Distillery
Ole Smoky Moonshine
Prichard's Distillery

Virginia
A. Smith Bowman Distillery
Catoctin Creek Distilling Company
Copper Fox Distillery
Virginia Distillery Co.

West Virginia
Smooth Ambler Spirits Co.

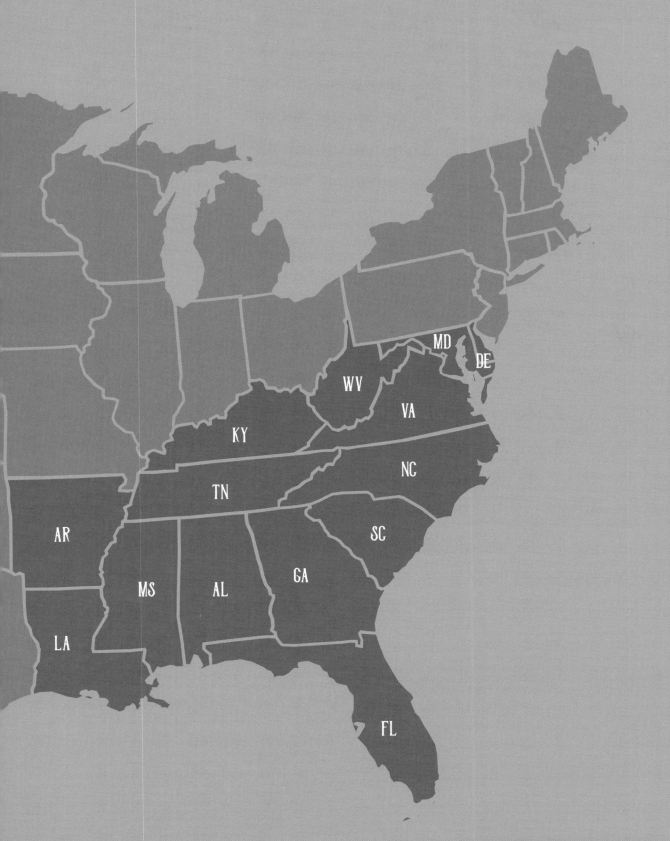

MIDWEST REGION DISTILLERIES

Illinois
FEW Spirits
KOVAL Distillery

Indiana
Bear Wallow Distillery
Midwest Grain Products (MGP)
Redemption Whiskey
This Is Stolen

Iowa
Cedar Ridge Winery & Distillery
Mississippi River Distilling Company
Templeton Rye

Michigan
Coppercraft Distillery
Journeyman Distillery
Traverse City Whiskey Co.
Two James Spirits

Nebraska
Cut Spike Distillery

Ohio
Cleveland Whiskey
Watershed Distillery

Wisconsin
Death's Door Spirits
Great Lakes Distillery
Yahara Bay Distillers

ND

SD

NE

KS

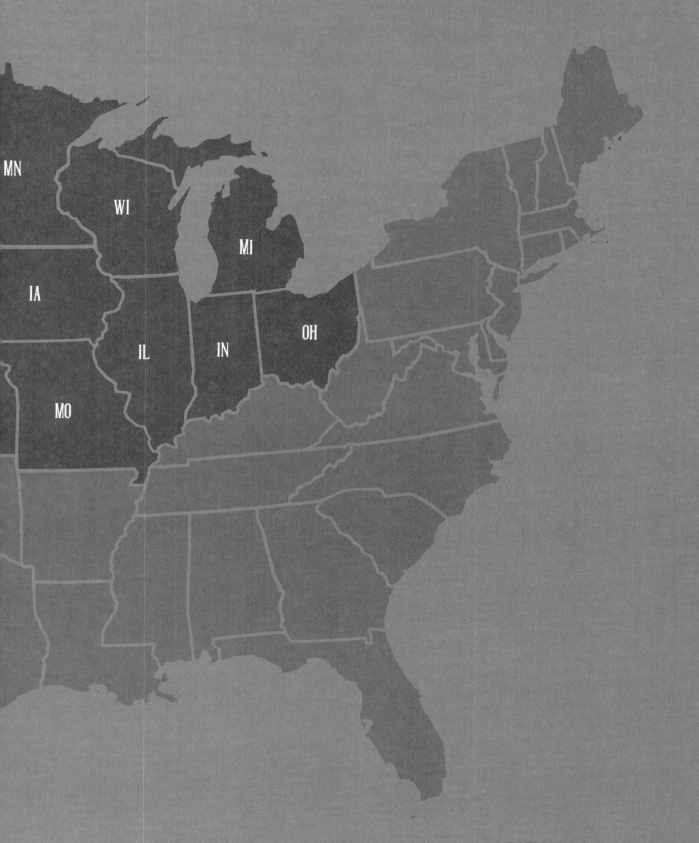

SOUTHWEST REGION DISTILLERIES

Arizona
Hamilton Distillers Inc.

New Mexico
Santa Fe Spirits

Texas
Balcones Distilling
Banner Distilling Company
Firestone & Robertson Distilling Co.
Garrison Brothers Distillery
Ranger Creek Brewing & Distilling
Treaty Oak Distilling
BENDT Distilling Co.
Yellow Rose Distilling

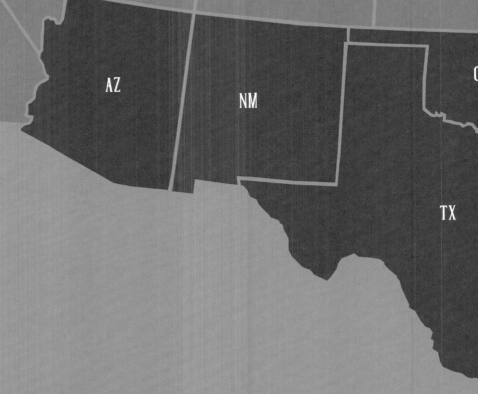

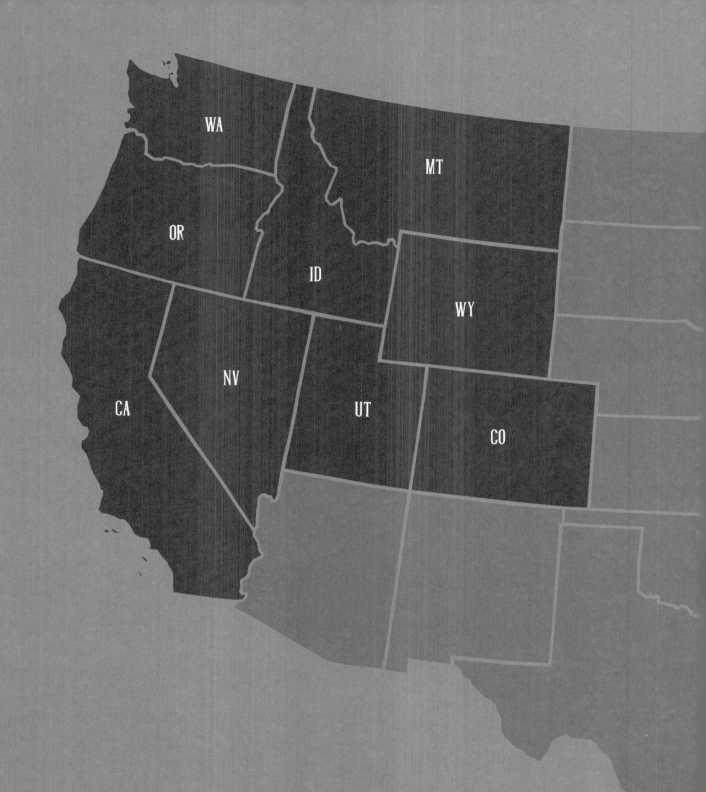

WESTERN REGION DISTILLERIES

California

Charbay Distillery
Hotaling & Co. Distillery
Sonoma Distilling Company
Spirit Works Distillery
Stark Spirits Distillery

Colorado

Distillery 291
10th Mountain Whiskey & Spirit Company
Colorado Gold Distillery
Laws Whiskey House
Leopold Bros. Distillery
Old Elk Distillery
Stranahan's Colorado Whiskey
Wood's High Mountain Distillery

Oregon

Deschutes Brewery & Bendistillery
Hood River Distillers/Clear Creek Distillery
House Spirits Distillery
Rogue Spirits Distillery

Utah

High West Distillery

Washington

Dry Fly Distilling
OOLA Distillery
Westland Distillery

Wyoming

Wyoming Whiskey

INDEX

ABOUT CIDER MILL PRESS
BOOK PUBLISHERS

Good ideas ripen with time. From seed to harvest, Cider Mill Press
brings fine reading, information, and entertainment together
between the covers of its creatively crafted books. Our Cider Mill
bears fruit twice a year, publishing a new crop of titles
each spring and fall.

"Where Good Books Are Ready for Press"

Visit us online at
cidermillpress.com
or write to us at
PO Box 454
12 Spring St.
Kennebunkport, Maine 04046